OLD SCHOOL
CHOPPERS

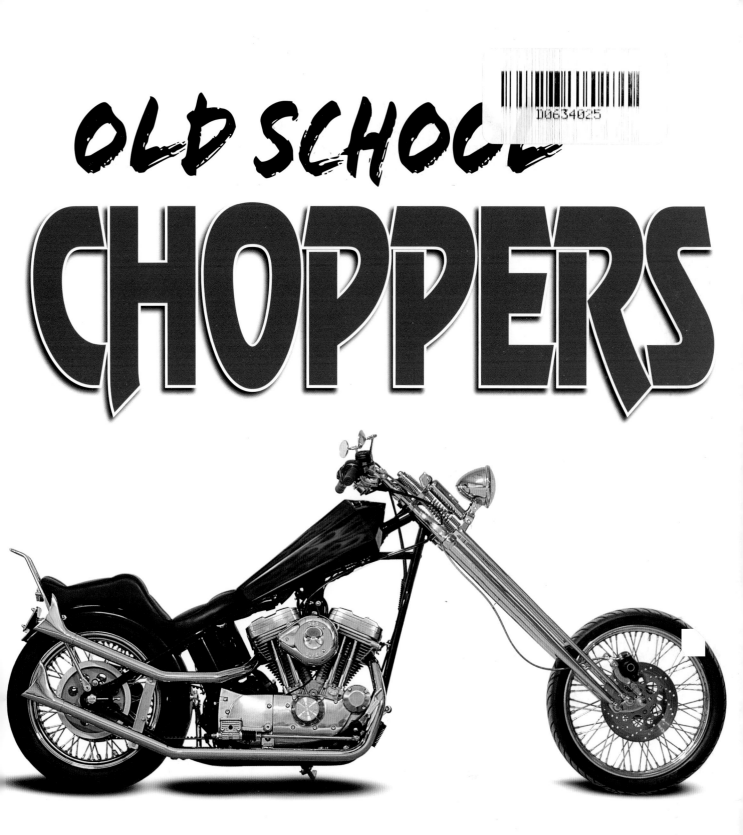

Alan Mayes

©2006 Alan Mayes
Published by

kp **krause publications**
An Imprint of F+W Publications

700 East State Street • Iola, WI 54990-0001
715-445-2214 • 888-457-2873

Our toll-free number to place an order or obtain
a free catalog is (800) 258-0929.

Library of Congress Catalog Number: 2006933681

ISBN 13-digit: 978-0-89689-246-0
ISBN 10-digit: 0-89689-246-8

Photo on page 1 courtesy of Paughco

Designed by Kay Sanders
Edited by Tom Collins

Printed in China

TABLE OF CONTENTS

Dedication

This book is dedicated to my dad, Lester J. Mayes. My dominant gearhead gene came from him.

Acknowledgments

I had lots of help in gathering the material for this book. I suppose it is possible to put together such a volume alone, but I would hate to attempt it. Thankfully, I didn't have to as my friends came through for me.

If there was one indispensable character in this whole undertaking, it was Dale Walksler. Dale is the owner/curator/chief mechanic/walking encyclopedia of Wheels Through Time All American Transportation Museum (WTTM) in Maggie Valley, North Carolina. Thirty-seven percent of the motorcycles featured individually in this book are Dale's.

When I traveled to Maggie Valley to shoot those bikes, he put me up in his cabin, shuffled the bikes in and out for me, started them up, raced across the parking lot and laid rubber on the floor inside. The good thing is that he was having at least as much fun as I was. It's an honor to call him friend.

Naturally I owe a debt of gratitude to the owners and/or builders of the other bikes featured herein. They are named individually in their respective chapters so I'll just acknowledge them as a group here. One *former* owner was of great help, though. That was Max Schmitt, the fine gent

who donated to WTTM the pearl white chopper that he and his dad built. He gave me a wealth of info on the bike.

Heartfelt thanks go to three individuals who provided priceless vintage photographs for inclusion in the historic sections of this book. They were Bob Clark, former editor of Street Chopper Magazine; Bo Huff, hot rod and custom car builder extraordinaire; and Steve Rebuck, active participant in the first round of chopper mania. Thankfully, they were wise enough to help document the history for the rest of us.

I also had a lot of help tracking down worthy bikes. That came in the form of Tommy Williams, Dana Mayes, Hackasaw, Kurt Morrow, Pat Patterson, and Roy Caruthers.

I also want to acknowledge my bosses/co-conspirators at *The Horse Back Street Choppers* magazine. Geno DiPol, Hank McQueeney, and Ralph "Hammer" Janus have given me the opportunity to work in the coolest job a gearhead could imagine having.

And to be honest, it's my affiliation with *The Horse* that provides the credibility to be offered the opportunity to write this book in the first place, so thanks my friends.

Alan Mayes

Introduction

Choppers are all the rage these days. Who doesn't want a chopper? Everyone knows someone who has a chopper, wants a chopper, is building a chopper, or is saving up to buy a chopper. One might think that it's all about the chopper in the two-wheeled world.

Choppers aren't anything new. The first chopper craze hit in the late 1960s and early 1970s. Just like today's saturation through television shows like the Discovery Channel's *American Chopper* and *Biker Build-Off*, back then we got a glimpse into the "chopper lifestyle" through cult movies like *The Wild Angels, Easy Rider,* and *Hell's Angels on Wheels* (to name only a few). But even then, the personalization of motorcycles was old hat.

The whole deal had really started 50 or more years before that round of motorcycle modifiers came on the scene. It was actually begun by those guys' grandfathers.

The first production motorcycles came about in the very early 20th century (Harley Davidson's official birth date is 1903). It's probably a safe bet that the first motorcycle modification occurred sometime within an hour of the first motorcycle arriving at the buyer's home!

Motorcycle guys cannot leave well enough alone. It's some kind of a genetic fault we all share.

The earliest customized bikes weren't choppers, though. They were what we call bobbers today. Stripped of everything not required to make the bike go and stop, they were made faster through weight reduction.

Gearheads... it's all about the gearheads. Motorcyclists, bikers, call us what you will. We are gearheads to the core and we have to tinker. It must be done. And it starts at an early age.

Even before we get actual motorized transport, we're making changes. How many stock bicycles remain from the years of your childhood? Not very many. Why? Because even at an early age, aspiring gearheads – future bikers – were modifying leg-powered bikes to make them look better, go faster, and sound better.

Sound better? Bicycles? Yes, sound better.

Why do you suppose there are so few Whitey Ford, Roger Maris, and Mickey Mantle baseball cards left? They got chewed up in bicycle spokes! We

Gearheads love all wheels. Bob Clark on his Triumph with a Deuce 5-window.

took Mom's clothespins and clipped the cards to our fender braces to make that cool motorcycle sound. Then we took off the fenders to make the bikes look even sleeker and more purposeful – bobber bicycles.

We had to improve the looks, too, at least in our own eyes. Twenty-twenty hindsight reveals those "improvements" might not have been all that effective. In 1964, I bought a brand new Schwinn Stingray-style bike from Sears. My paper route earnings couldn't absorb buying a real Stingray. The bike was a beautiful metallic gold color, which I promptly painted over with brushed-on maroon Western Auto enamel. Dad was livid, but I had personalized my bike to make it my own.

I was a conservative participant in the first chopper faze of the 1960s, at least in heart. In 1969 I bought a brand new BSA that promptly received a lime green metalflake paint job and gave up its front fender to the cause. The eight-inch AEE slugs that I bought were thankfully never installed. The horror stories about broken slugs prevented that.

Our bikes are bigger and they're all self-propelled now, but we haven't changed much. We still have to personalize them. Most of us have no idea what happened to those old bicycles of our youth. The motorcycles that followed might be a little easier to track down in some cases.

Some people's old bikes are real easy to track down, in fact. A few of them have survived intact to this day. Those form the nucleus of the array of bikes shown in this book.

What we have assembled here is a cross section of bobbers and choppers. They range in age from over 80 years old to about three years old. There are 30 motorcycles featured individually in 28 chapters. Fourteen are classified as bobbers and the others are choppers. A couple of them could have gone either way in the classification process.

Two were built by one of the masters of the previous chopper craze, Minnesota's Donnie Smith. He's still going strong, by the way. Talent and taste have staying power. Most of the rest were built by their owners.

A few were built by small shops that have the good taste to build what looks right and traditional, never mind what the fad of the day is. Those bikes will look as good 30 years from now as they do today. They would have looked great 30 years ago, too.

What they all share in common is that they are what I think fits the term "old school." That is a term that has been bandied about by the clueless for so long that it has no discernable official meaning anymore, but it's a popular term and one that at least gets people's attention, so we've used it in the title of the book.

Except for the Crocker, each one of these bikes existed in another form at some time in its life. It was modified into the bike we see today. If it's a bobber, it was cut down to increase performance and/or create a pleasing minimalist style. If it's a chopper, its builder took a stock motorcycle and modified it to meet his particular vision of what a motorcycle should look like.

You may note that the majority of these motorcycles are Harley Davidsons. That wasn't intentional, but that's how it would play out for anyone's chopper and bobber book unless he specifically excluded them.

There are also a couple of Indians and some British bikes, specifically Triumphs and two Ariel Square Fours. The Ariels were a coup in my eyes. Most surviving Ariels are stockers and they are highly sought after by restorers of British motorcycles. To have two modified Ariels in the same book is rare indeed. I have personally wanted one for years but one that I can afford coming along at the time I have some available money hasn't occurred yet. I still hold hope, though.

Bobbers or choppers, whichever your preference, the motorcycles assembled here are fine examples of the breed. They are not assembly line bikes built to the latest fad or to some corporate committee's idea of what they should be.

Each one is as individual as the man who built it. I would love to own each and every one. In a truly just world, I would.

—Alan Mayes

SECTION ONE:

HISTORICAL PERSPECTIVE

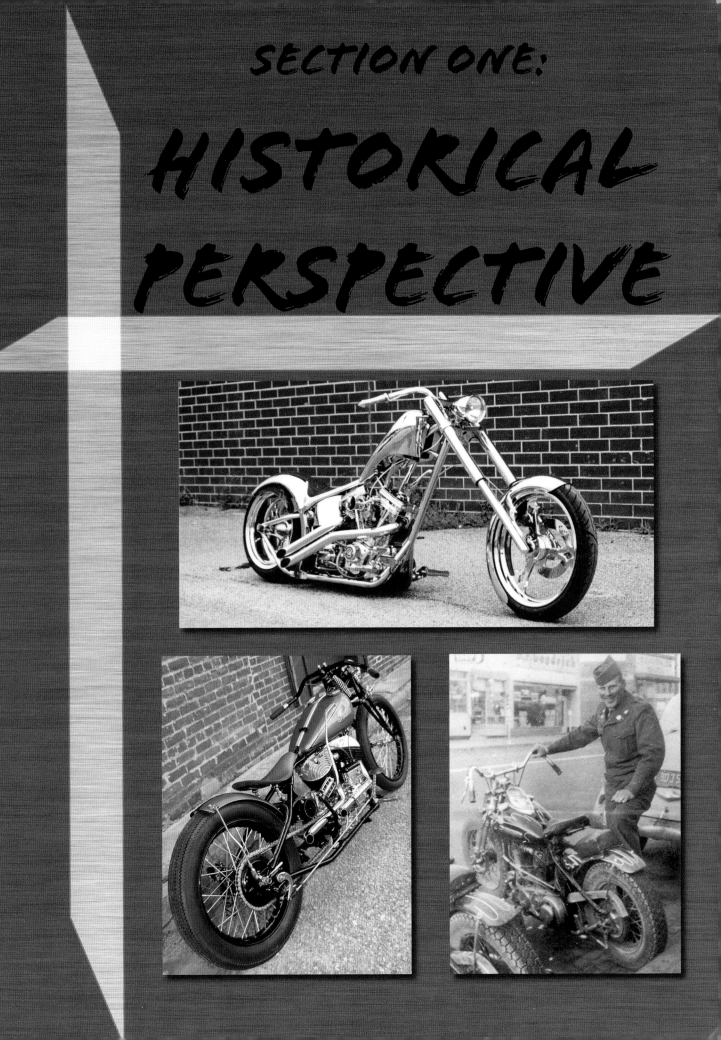

1966 Shovelhead engine powers this chopper in a modified Harley frame.

Steve Rebuck photo

What's It All Mean?

Bobber, chopper - what's the difference anyway?

Sometimes these days, the terms are used interchangeably, though it is incorrect to do so. The confusion probably stems from the recent popularity of customized motorcycles in the television and print media and the fact that lots and lots of people who do not have any background in things mechanical at all have become overnight chopper fans. These newbies often fail to recognize the differences in types and even brands of motorcycles.

Bob Clark Collection photo

It's not just in types of bikes either. For someone not really familiar with motorcycle nuances, a V-twin Honda or Suzuki might look the same or very similar to a Harley Davidson or S&S-powered cruiser. To a Harleyphile, the differences between a Panhead and a Shovelhead are completely obvious; not so to the uninitiated.

Once explained, the differences between choppers and bobbers are easy to comprehend. Earliest bobbers also predate the first choppers by at least 50 years, so it's easy to understand the thinking behind the two different styles.

Think of choppers as a latter day variation on the bobber theme. Rather than try to give a complete history, though, we'll just hit some highlights and point you in the direction of some superb examples and sources of both.

Bobbers

For a couple of the motorcycles featured in this book, the term "bobber" is actually being applied retroactively. That's because when those bikes came to be in the 1920s and 1930s, the name hadn't been coined yet. The concept was there, but not the name.

Bobbers as we know them actually came to popularity in the period immediately following World War II. Returning servicemen had pocketfuls of unspent pay and a yen for some homegrown excitement. Many had been exposed during the war to the riding thrills afforded by motorcycles. World War II had marked the U.S. Army's first *real* foray into two-wheeled military vehicles.

Because of their quickness, maneuverability, and fuel economy, the bikes provided by Harley Davidson and Indian had proven to be worthy partners in the Allied victories. The British Army had used Triumphs and BSAs with the same success.

So, all of a sudden the soldiers were home and there were thousands of military surplus motorcycles available, in addition to the used civilian bikes already on the market. Motorcycles were cheap, plentiful and thrilling. They were also a little underpowered for the average thrill-seeking G.I. He had just returned from facing death on a daily basis. A slow putt in the park wasn't going to cut it for long.

Many credit returning WWII soldiers with creating bobbers.
Mac photo

As early as the 1920s bobbers existed in form, if not in name.

All types of early racing bikes doubled as street bikes, too.

Now we all know that performance is a matter of power-to-weight ratio. The easiest way to make a stock motorcycle faster? Make it lighter. That's just what those guys in the '40s did. Steel front fenders weigh a lot. In the trash bin with them! Footboards weigh more than pegs. Off with the boards! Some bit of rear fender is probably necessary to keep mud off your back, but about half of what the factory provided will do nicely. Bob it!

Did you say "bob?" Bob – bobber – the bobber was born. If it wasn't necessary to make the bike go or stop, it wasn't necessary period. All of a sudden, the bikers of the day had faster motorcycles and it hadn't cost them an extra penny. Of course that still wasn't enough, so they made engine improvements and gearing changes, but the bobber as we know it had been born.

Flashback-back-back-back

Motorcycles have been raced ever since there were two motorcycles in the same town. That goes back to very early in the 20th century. Not too long after those first two guys raced, sanctioned racing came about, because we need to have rules for everything. The Federation of American Motorcyclists, which eventually grew into the American Motorcycle Association (today's American Motorcyclist Association), had classes for all types of racing. Whether racing in hill climbs, board tracks, cross-country or on dirt tracks, motorcycle racing was everywhere in the 1920s and 1930s.

We are a fairly rich society these days and it's not unusual for one family to have several specialized vehicles. Multiple motorcycles sharing the same garage might include a touring bike, a chopper, a

By the early 1950s, motorcycles were getting a little more specialized.

couple of antiques, and a dirt bike, each one serving a specific niche purpose.

That was not the case 70 or 80 years ago. First of all, there weren't that many different types of motorcycles and, even if there had been, the average rider could not have afforded to own more than one. So, Joe Earlyrider had one bike that met all his needs, including daily transportation back and forth to work. If his "needs" included racing, his bike was set up to do that since racing was the most demanding and specialized use of the bike.

All his other transportation needs were met with the race bike, which was actually a modified road bike with the front fender, floorboards, lights, and battery removed. The rear fender was bobbed to a minimal useful size. The bike was the pre-bobber bobber.

Bobbers-the minimalist motorcycles

Bobbers appeal to the minimalist in all of us. They are motorcycles at their most basic. Engine,

frame, two wheels, a gas tank and a small place to sit – that's about the extent of a bobber. Everything else only exists to tie those few basics together. Their style exists in their simplicity. Little or no decoration beyond chrome rims and a shiny paint job; short wheelbase that is just long enough to accommodate the powertrain and the frame of its owner.

Built to go fast and handle the curves, a bobber might weigh as much as 200 pounds less than the production bike it was based on, depending on the make and model. That's a significantly lighter load for a given engine to propel. It also makes for more responsive handling and enhanced braking.

Choppers

Who knew? How could we have known that what was once considered avant-garde 30-plus years ago would become mainstream? Choppers are now the motorized objects of affection for America's newest love affair with self-propelled conveyances.

Utilizing a 1952 Harley frame, this bike was built with a 1969 Shovelhead engine.
Steve Rebuck photo

Back in the mid-1960s to mid-1970s, choppers enjoyed their first wave of popularity. But things were much different then. In those days, reasons for building choppers had a rebellious root. Foremost seemed to be non-conformity. While Joe Average was learning to "meet the nicest people on a Honda," Benny Badass was trying to convince those same folks that he was *not* one of those nice people.

Benny did that by making his bike as wild and different as he could. Changes included radically raking the front end, then extending the front forks at least two inches longer than anyone else had done. Hang a sissy bar out back and spray on some metalflake paint, and *voila*, two-wheeled individuality was born.

The vision of choppers was etched into young heads through movies like *Easy Rider*, *Wild Angels*, and others. With the exception of *ER*, those formula B-flicks usually showed gangs of wild bikers terrorizing the countryside on their noisy, usually dirty, choppers. They were the epitome of non-conformity, causing grandmas and children alike to shake in their shoes.

One of the premier companies in the first chopper wave was AEE Choppers.
Bob Clark Collection photo

Magazines like *Street Chopper*, *Custom Chopper*, *Easyriders*, *Chopper Guide*, and many others sprang up to feed the frenzy over choppers. That only two of those original titles survive today, albeit in much different form, is testament to the fickle nature of the motorcycling public.

Fast forward nearly 40 years and choppers are in vogue again. Or at least motorcycles that are *called* choppers are. Even such straight-laced entities as the Discovery Channel are now associated with the bikes. In fact, credit the Discovery Channel for much of the chopper's move to Main Street.

Their two series, *American Chopper* and *Biker Build-Off*, have enjoyed phenomenal acceptance and have helped to propel names like Indian Larry, Billy Lane, Paul Teutel (junior and senior), and Jesse James to national attention. Even those who have never ridden a motorcycle, or even shown any interest in them, know who these guys are.

Directly opposite from the early chopper riders and builders, many of today's "chopper" fans dig them because they are the "in" thing. What was once a rebellion has now become a mainstream gathering. Thousands of 401k funds have been cashed in to buy a custom motorcycle.

There are a couple of funny things about today's chopper phase. One is that most hardcore traditional chopper guys are not involved in it. There are a few notable exceptions to that, but for the most part, *longtime* chopper riders are pretty much ignoring the current chopper craze, or at least shaking their heads at it. Many anxiously await the day when the fad ends and bikers are once again outcasts. Ahh, those were the good old days.

The second point is really much to blame for the first. The motorcycles being built today and called "choppers" are not really choppers in the strictest sense. They are new bikes assembled in a chopper *style*. Nothing was chopped; hence, they are not technically choppers. Sorry, French fries that are baked in the oven are not French fries, either. They're baked French-cut potatoes, potatoes that *look* like French fries.

And therein lies the rub. Old school chopper guys don't build new bikes from all-new components, buying a frame here, an engine there, fenders and gas tank from another catalog. Such bikes are custom bikes but not choppers. *Real* choppers are made from existing motorcycles that have been… that's right, chopped!

This is a beautiful bike, but it's not a chopper. No motorcycle was harmed in building it!

Custom car guru Bo Huff built this 1947 HD Knucklehead in the late 1960s.
Bo Huff photo

Early choppers were fashioned by heavily modifying stock, existing motorcycles. Frames were raked in the garage by cutting behind the neck and fabricating new pieces to fill in the gap. Forks were extended by making new tubes and fitting them to the existing triple trees. Sometimes they were made with solid front tubes and no suspension. The old days weren't necessarily smarter!

Before a bike was (is) chopped, though, it is usually bobbed. That is, the unnecessary components are taken off and discarded. Front fenders, turn signals, long back fenders, etc. They all get the pitch or the axe, just like on a bobber.

There were many other things done back in the old days that are thankfully not being repeated these days by savvy builders. One of those was the use of

Chopper riders stopped for a break during a 1968 Southern California ride.
Bob Clark Collection photo

Steve Rebuck's chopper started life as a 1968 Harley Police Special.
Steve Rebuck photo

slugs to extend forks. One of the cheap ways to make a front end longer was to add slugs to the top legs of a telescopic fork.

Basically, these were just machined metal pieces, offered in various lengths, which screwed onto the top of the fork tube, lengthening it by the given amount. Want to extend the front end by 10 inches? Screw in a set of 10-inch slugs. Slugs were offered by companies such as Tom and Rose McMullen's AEE Choppers for everything from Harley Davidsons to BSAs, Triumphs, Honda 450s, and just about any other bike you can think of.

They were extremely unsafe, especially in lengths that exceeded the distance between the upper and lower triple clamps. Stories were rampant about someone riding his bike along at a fair clip, only to have the slug break, usually at the base of the threads. The results could be fatal.

The aforementioned one-piece tubes were famous for failure, too. See, the styles one could get by with on smooth California freeways could prove to be unwise designs on a frost-heave pot-holed chunk of Michigan or New Jersey byway. Long, bouncy front

This chopper is typical of those from the late 1960s and early 1970s.
Bob Clark Collection photo

Even in the early 1970s, builders recognized the advantage of Honda 750 power.
Bob Clark Collection photo

ends have been known to snap in two, or at least fold in half, when the front tire fell into a chuckhole.

While we're on the subject of front ends, a couple of styles popular in the early days were springers and girders. Aside from their aesthetic beauty, springers were popular because they were plentiful. Remember, 1930s and 1940s Harleys and Indians were only 25 to 40 years old then, the equivalent of a mid-1960s to early 1980s bike today, not all that old. They were also fairly easy to make or to modify for someone with some mechanical and welding skills.

The same holds true with girders. The early chopper magazines had many advertisements for girder and springer front forks built in someone's backyard garage "factory." Though some girders and springers of the day, such as the ones built by Durfee and by Smith Brothers & Fetrow, were well engineered and built with quality and safety in mind (and are sought out today by traditional chopper builders), some others were less than safe. Reports of broken welds and riders catapulted over handlebars were not uncommon.

By the mid-1970s, choppers were getting glitzy, some with gold plating and lots of engraved parts.
Bob Clark Collection photo

In 1979, Raja the painter and former Street Chopper editor Bob Clark hammed it up at the Movieland Wax Museum.
Bob Clark Collection photo

What was extremely different about building a chopper back then was that only a minimum number of aftermarket parts existed, at least compared to today's huge market. And that's how the term "chopper" really got its origin. Guys had to *chop* their stock bikes to get the look they wanted.

Originally, there were no custom frame manufacturers, so the idea of stretching and raking a frame meant the ol' hacksaw and welder were employed. Around the end of the 1960s and beginning of the 1970s, some companies started to build custom frames that utilized the look chopper builders were after. Such names as Santee, Paughco, Amen, and a few others come to mind.

Santee and Paughco are still in business and still building excellent frames. Many recently built choppers and bobbers utilize their frames, front ends and more. The name Amen is still alive, too, but with a different direction of building mostly high-dollar, very low-slung customs.

In 1968, bobbed fenders were just that, stock fenders that had been cut shorter, bobbed. Although there are chopper purists still doing that, the more common origin of a so-called bobbed fender now is a catalog. New fender, pre-bobbed, made in Taiwan.

Early choppers often wore a combination of parts that may have come from several different motorcycles.

A frame from one bike, say a 1940s Harley Knucklehead, may have been mated to an engine from another, like a late 1950s Panhead. A springer off a 1938 bike may have been extended 14 inches in the garage. A ribbed fender from the neighbor's Triumph was then shortened and painted to match the tank off of Uncle Louie's Mustang. A chopper was born.

Yes, boys and girls, there actually was a motorcycle called the Mustang. And many of those humble little bikes donated their gas tanks to the first chopper craze. They were so popular that Paughco and some others still make reproduction versions. Many chopper builders have a Mustang tank in the attic awaiting the next project bike.

Schools

But enough of the past. What about "choppers" of today? There are actually a couple of different schools of thought on choppers today. For want of better terms, we'll call them Old School and New School although I hate those names because they are confusing – or confused. I don't know which. Maybe I'm the one that's confused.

New School first. Into this group I would throw all the bikes that are choppers in name only. Lump the boys from Orange County Choppers, the dozens of small builders around the country turning out new chopper-styled bikes, and the "production" chopper builders (an oxymoron if there ever was one) like American IronHorse, Big Dog, and Swift.

These bikes are, in almost every example, brand-new bikes built from brand-new components in a style reminiscent of choppers. That is, they have long front ends and raked frames, usually stretched in the backbone and downtube. The majority of these bikes are built from catalog parts, starting with a catalog frame carrying a Manufacturer's Statement of Origin (MSO). To that the assembler will have usually added a catalog tank, either from the frame manufacturer or another company. From another source will come a front end.

Wheels and engine will usually come from other various sources. In the case of the individual builder or small shop, these bikes will have to be registered as "special build" or "assembly" or something similar, depending on the state where the bike is registered.

Another twist on this formula exists. It is possible to buy a chopper kit bike from companies like Bikers' Choice and Drag Specialties that includes everything needed to build a rideable, running "chopper" but the gasoline. Some kits even include the oil and brake fluid. All you do is bolt it together and paint it (in theory it's that easy, anyway).

The factory-built bikes like American IronHorse, Big Dog, and several others will actually have an MSO that carries the manufacturer's name and will be registered as that brand of bike. As stated before, these motorcycles are not choppers in the strictest sense of the term. They are, however, what the motorcycle newcomers and Discovery Channel watchers think of when someone mentions the term "chopper."

Old School choppers are a different animal altogether. These are bikes being built in much the same way bikes were built 30 to 40 years ago. The builders of these bikes gather parts from swap meets, junkyards, buddies' garages, eBay (a huge, global swap meet), their own donor bikes and local dealers' back rooms. Then they fabricate mounts, cut here, weld there and make things work together that don't usually belong together. The result is often a bike that is very distinctive and unlike any other.

Nothing beats tooling down the highway on a chopper you've built yourself - nothing.
Bob Clark Collection photo

These bikes create two different reactions in those who first see them. They cause gearheads with an eye for creativity to smile. They cause the fans of new school bikes to turn away, looking for something more shiny and expensive.

That brings us to another differentiator in the New School/Old School discussion. Though it seems extreme, one of the New School Orange County Choppers bikes recently sold through Sam's Club (yes, that Sam's Club) for $137,000. To be fair, that price included a weekend for two in New York City, so let's say $130,000 for the bike.

Yeah, one bike! Reportedly, some of the theme bikes that have been featured on the TV show actually cost over $250,000! So-called production choppers can easily run in the $30,000+ range, give or take five grand, depending on options.

A small custom builder in the Midwest recently built a beautiful Old School bike by gathering parts from the various aforementioned sources. It has an engine that he built himself from purchased components, a swap meet frame, and various parts from old bikes, tractors, and cars. He plans to sell the bike for $36,000. He confided to me that he has $6,500 invested in it. Professionally built bikes are costing many times what a real chopper should cost to build.

There is another group of builders that is somewhat in between the Old School and New School. Let's call it Middle School, or maybe Reform School.

The most famous of these among the currently movie-star-popular builders are Billy Lane and Jesse James. Either of these fairly young builders has the ability to personally fabricate almost any component on one of their motorcycle creations, and they often do. Both know their way around a planishing hammer, an English wheel, and any other fabricating utensil you can name.

They can build flashy, New School bikes with the best of them, winning build-offs and wooing fans begging to be deemed worthy to buy one of their customs. But for themselves, for their own use, they usually go with an Old School style of bike. The late Indian Larry fit this niche as well except that he didn't bother to build the new-style bikes at all.

There are really so many different types of motorcycles, such varied tastes, and so many opposing opinions that it is really difficult to try to define what makes something Old School or New School or any other category. Smarter men and women than I have tried to do so with limited success. Considering it from that point of view, I don't know why my opinions would be any better received. Forget I said anything.

SECTION TWO:
BOBBERS

1924 California Cutdown

Boys and girls, this is a genuine, unmolested, original Harley-Davidson "bobber" and it's more than 80 years old. This is a perfect example of where bobbers came from... and why they came to be.

Bobbers were (and still are) bobbed production motorcycles. Absolutely everything that wasn't necessary to make the motorcycle go or stop was removed. Fenders and lights weigh a certain number of pounds. Removing those pounds makes the bike go faster without doing anything to the engine. It's simple math, power-to-weight ratio.

This 1924 JDCA is a rare, make that very rare, survivor. It belongs to Dale Walksler of the Wheels Through Time All-American Transportation

Museum in Maggie Valley, North Carolina. Dale has been collecting Harley-Davidsons and other vintage American motorcycles for more than 30 years, since way before it was fashionable to do so.

He is thankfully wise enough to know when he has a gem in hand and is not even remotely tempted to restore such a wonderfully original piece of motorcycle history.

In the 1920s, motorcyclists did not have the plethora of different specialized models that exists today. At one time early in this bike's life, an owner stripped the bike to its bare essentials for the likely purpose of dashing across the California desert in competition with like-minded individuals.

The handlebars reflect the modifications present on such bikes as well.

The JDCA model designation indicates that this particular motorcycle came from the factory as a 74-cubic-inch version, fitted with aluminum pistons and a full electrical system. Somewhere over the years, it was fitted with a Bosch magneto. This bike also has the Harley Ricardo heads.

The carburetor is an original style Schebler pulling air through a stock air cleaner. How many of those can there be in the world? The rest of the engine is fairly stock. It feeds power to a three-speed transmission with jockey shift and standard foot clutch. WTTM is known as "the museum that runs" and the California Cutdown is one of the bikes that runs well and runs often.

In keeping with the lighter-is-better mantra, there is no front fender and the gas tank has been shortened. The rear fender is from a 1913 HD. Note the pin striping still showing on the gas tank and also that there is almost no paint left on the frame anymore.

This is a bike that had a hard life in the past, but was thankfully kept intact. It's in loving hands now, but it still gets a chance to throw a little gravel once in a while.

Slim profile, the better to dodge cactus with, my dear.

Stripped and ready for action, a 1924 California Cutdown.

This bike started life as a 1924 Harley JDCA.

This 1924 bobber is delightfully complete.

The shortened gas tank shows well-earned battle scars.

Bike usually starts in less than three kicks.

1928 Harley Two-Cam

By 1928, Harley-Davidson had been running twin-cam engines in race bikes for several years. Harley's road machine buyers were clamoring for more power and speed from their motorcycles.

The factory responded by introducing two-cam versions of both the 61-cubic-inch and 74-cubic-inch engines. It's a certain example of racing improving the breed. This bike is one of the 74-inch JDH models.

Says owner Dale Walksler, "This old period bobber I purchased apart from Scooter in Ohio. It is a stroker two-cam motor by Mike Lange. The frame is NOS with original paint. This bike would have been used as a TT special."

As Dale notes, it is now a stroker; an 88-cubic-inch stroker to be precise. It uses a set of 1929 heads, the standard issue Schebler carb and air cleaner.

Part of the Two Cam package when introduced was the use of domed magnesium alloy (Dow Metal) pistons. The resultant higher compression ratio produced better performance. Motorcycles were getting pretty sophisticated compared to just a few years prior.

Harley was also striving to make the motorcycles more trouble-free and safer to ride. The 1928 models featured a throttle-controlled oil pump to help with lubrication chores. Those models also featured a standard front brake for the first time.

Given the weak nature of rear drum brakes at that time, imagine what it would have been like to ride a bike with *only* a rear brake! The addition of a rudimentary front binder was surely a welcome gesture to riders of the day.

This bike has an accessory speedometer by Corbin. The seat is from an Indian of a similar vintage and the rear fender is actually a 1925 Harley front fender. It also has a Bosch magneto and it wears period racing exhaust pipes.

The bike is stripped for racing action.

Stock round tube springer still works great.

This 1928 Two-Cam Harley bobber was a TT bike.

The Two-Cam engine houses domed Dow Metal pistons.

Corbin speedo was a period accessory.

Some racers carried spare spark plugs in the handlebar ends.

A three-speed tank-mounted shifter.

Handle on fender assists in getting bike onto stand.

1937 Harley UMG TT Special Bobber

Despite the fact that the new one-year-old OHV Knucklehead was winning lots of fans in 1937, Harley's side valve models were still their bread and butter and lots of them found their way into garages and carports across the US.

Quite a bit of grassroots and factory racing research had been put into the old style engines and the old tricks still worked for the Harley owner seeking some increased performance from the V-twin mill.

Dale Walksler built this black beauty from parts in 1999, starting his collection with the right case and the rare cam cover. It's a fairly unusual UMG model, not even listed in some Harley reference books. According to one source, the designation means that is was originally a 74-cubic-inch, Bosch magneto model.

The engine in this one now displaces 80 cubes, though. It has an M51 Linkert carburetor and a

1936 UL air cleaner. Gus Karnes custom-made the exhaust, a good-looking high/low trumpet end set-up. And, yes, it sounds at least as good as it looks.

The year 1937 saw several upgrades to the larger (74 and 80) side valve models, including the Knuckle's horseshoe oil tank and gas tank instrumentation. Most welcome was the four-speed transmission replacing the old three-speed unit.

As he usually does, Dale Walksler placed his own touch on this bike. He builds them to ride, so he makes sure they perform and that they suit his fancy. He also does them period correct, the way an owner in 1937 would have done.

In this case, that meant building it as a TT special and doing a few little things that would have made the bike more suitable for such competition. Things like raising the transmission an extra inch for clearance, for instance. It also has slightly taller 19-

If there was ever a perfect 1937 bobber, this is it.

Rear fender is a bobbed military fender.

Dale's UMG sports dual shifters.

Military fork and 19-inch wheel help ground clearance.

Flanders bars and a stock HD headlight.

Period custom Sparto taillight.

Gus Karnes formed the custom trumpet exhaust.

The 80-cubic-inch side valve was still a potent performer.

inch wheels, again offering a little more ground clearance. Two-inch longer military forks help to accomplish the same goal.

The raised transmission means less clearance for the oil tank, so this bike has a slightly shorter one. The taillight is Sparto-style cast aluminum. The bike has modified military style fenders front and rear. The handlebars are from Flanders. Tires are by Firestone. The gorgeous black paint was sprayed by Gene Welch.

Dale says the bike has literally been ridden thousands of miles. It's a beautiful period-correct version of what a bright and shiny near new Harley bobber would have been back in late 1930s and early 1940s. No wonder bobbers were so popular.

Lucky Dog's 1939 Harley EL Bobber

Some guys have all the luck…
Some guys do nothing but complain

With apologies to Rod Stewart, that was the scene in Maggie Valley, North Carolina, on the November 2005 day that Jim "Mr. Lucky" Usher's winning ticket was drawn for the annual Wheels Through Time Museum's bike raffle.

Jim won this fabulous "new" 1939 EL Knucklehead bobber and smiled all the way back home to Eastaboga, Alabama. The rest of us complained and the complaining hasn't died down much since then!

Dale Walksler completely built this his '39 Knuck in the WTTM restoration shop behind the museum. The museum raffles off a motorcycle each year to

raise funds for improvements to the facility's displays. This 2005 prize proved to be one of the most sought-after yet.

The 1939 EL Knuck is the 61-cubic-inch version. This bike's motor is all 1939 with the small port heads. Dale says the cases were found in Doby Reed's junk pile.

When new, the EL sold for $435. Of course that's in 1939 dollars. Just a simple paint job costs way more than that now.

Speaking of paint jobs, the burgundy and white version on this '39 was laid down by Gene Welch. Other than the Dave Butcher leather seat on the stock pan, Dale did all the rest of the work on this baby. It took him a total of four months. Talented chap, is he not?

The engine was rebuilt in the WTTM fashion, making it a one or two kick starter. The carb is an

The 1939 Knuckle was a raffle prize in 2005.

The front end is a stock HD springer.

The pretty exhaust system is by Gerald Rinehart.

The 61-cubic-inch Knuckle engine.

M55 Linkert using a 1936 Harley air cleaner. A battery ignition keeps things lit. The exhaust is a fine looking, finer sounding Rinehart system.

The bike uses a stock 1941 Knucklehead frame. To that is attached a stock Harley springer front end. Wheels and tires at both ends of the bike are 18-inch stock wires shod with Coker tires.

Well, at least Jim Usher seemed to appreciate his prize when he got it. And since the raffle ticket was only $10, surely he'll be willing to sell it some day and double his money!

This knuckle uses a tank mounted four speed shifter.

Mirror was kept in close, and down low.

Seat leather work was done by Dave Butcher on an original seat pan.

Everything is beautiful,
including the springer fork.

1940 Crocker "Factory Bobber"

Few motorcycles will get a true biker's blood warm like a Crocker. Brand loyalty goes out the window when a Crocker is in the vicinity. Harley lovers, Indian fans, British bike aficionados, it doesn't matter. Everyone who knows about Crockers lusts after them.

And why not?

In the strictest sense, Dale Walksler's 1940 Crocker isn't really a bobber. Like Jessica Rabbit, it was "drawn that way." Crockers were stripped-down lightweight rockets from the factory. They were hand-built, each to the customer's specification, so it's highly possible that, except for a few sold to the Arizona Highway Patrol, no two were exactly alike.

Antique motorcycle people often refer to the Crocker as the Duesenberg of American motorcycles. The comparison is warranted.

Like the Duesenbergs of the 1920s and 1930s, street model Crockers were big and powerful, hand built and perfectly finished. They utilized the best components of the day and they were beautifully styled. One cannot be in the presence of either and not be impressed.

Al Crocker

The genius behind Crocker motorcycles was Albert Crocker, who started his motorcycle career in the 1910s with the Thor Motorcycle firm. He later held positions as a dealer and sales representative for Indian, ultimately winding up in 1928 as the Indian dealer for Los Angeles.

The perfect bobber – from a small factory 70 years ago.

Crocker's distinctive taillight.

Local engineer Paul Bigsby and Crocker joined forces to build speedway bikes, first with V-twin Indian engines and eventually with their own design OHV 500 cc singles. The speedway racers did well for awhile, but were eventually overtaken by the JAP-powered (that's John Alfred Prestwick, not an ethnic slur) British machines.

Crocker turned away from race bikes and decided to build his own road-going V-twin hot rods. The lessons of the racing bikes followed him to his new venture. The engines and transmissions were strong with heavy duty castings and the best materials, including liberal usage of aluminum.

This kept the weight low and the powerful engines offered a substantial power-to-weight ratio that neither Indian nor Harley-Davidson could match.

The Crocker street twins hit the market in 1936, just a few short months before Harley-Davidson introduced the venerable Knucklehead. Both engines had a displacement of 61-cubic-inches (1,000 cc), but the Harley weighed about 80 pounds more than the Crocker and had at least 10 fewer horsepower. There was no comparison in street performance.

Factory stock Crockers were capable of cruising speeds of 90 to 100 miles per hour and had a top speed of over 110. Remember, that was in 1936. The compression ratio was only about 7:1. Those performance numbers are almost exactly the same as a current Harley Sportster with a 1,200 cc engine and 9:1 compression. The Crocker's 70-year-old numbers are impressive indeed.

It was a factory-produced rocket.

The name that sent fear into the hearts of H-D and Indian owners 70 years ago.

Person's King Comfort seat

Al Crocker was pretty sure of himself regarding the performance of his motorcycles. He offered a full purchase price refund to any Crocker owner who was beaten by a stock Indian or Harley-Davidson. Reportedly, he never had to write a check for such a purpose.

Still, it was hard then as now for a small manufacturer to compete with the larger ones. The Crocker bikes were superior in performance and many will say in build quality, too. But the economies of scale between a large and small company are huge.

The standard Crockers sold for about $150 more than the comparable competition and yet Crocker reportedly lost $2,500 on each one. Bleeding from that size of a wound cannot last forever. Crocker production ceased at the beginning of World War II.

Experts say fewer than 100 were built. Of those, perhaps 30 complete machines exist today. Dale Walksler owns two – a single cylinder speedway bike and this 1940 street bike.

Dale Walksler's 1940

Dale Walksler rides his Crocker almost every day. It is a rare trip to his Wheels Through Time Museum that is not accompanied by the sound of that gorgeous Crocker hemi-headed V-twin being kicked to life.

The gravel parking lot is strafed with signs of gravel thrown from the rear wheel as Dale shows off for museum visitors. An equal number of black marks adorn the concrete floor in front of the museum's "bobber display" where the bike has been started

No babying for this baby – she gets ridden hard.

The view from the rider's seat.

(usually one kick does it) and peeled down the aisle for another trip outside numerous times.

The ruggedness of the Crocker design is evident in this machine. It's almost 70 years old and is never babied, other than regular routine maintenance. Yet it runs flawlessly and starts every time. Dale has even drag raced this aged beauty, turning a very respectable 16 second quarter at 83 mph.

It is also one of the most beautiful machines you could ever hope to lay eyes on. The castings are nearly flawless and are polished, but not overly so. The right side case is engine-turned aluminum. This is one of only about 15 hemi-headed Crocker engines produced. Some of the early hemi versions had cracking problems, so the design was dropped. Dale says that only three or four remain now.

The engine on this bike retains its original 61-cubic-inch displacement, though there was ample room in the Crocker design for boring the cylinders out substantially. Johnny Eagles assembled this engine. The three-speed transmission shifts flawlessly.

The ignition is by way of an Edison Splitdorf magneto. The carburetor is a Linkert M5. Flanders handlebars are employed as is a stock Persons King Comfort seat.

This particular bike has the smaller, approximately two-gallon cast aluminum gas tank. The tank and the other sheetmetal are finished in midnight blue and accented with red and gold. A larger three-and-one-half gallon tank was also offered. The paint was done by Richard Morris, who also assembled the bike when it was restored.

Hot Rod Done Right

Crockers like this one are a real inspiration to custom bike builders today. Even the best-known and most skilled look at a Crocker like this one with admiration. Albert Crocker had a keen eye for design style and proportion. The best-looking modern custom-built bobbers bear a striking resemblance to a 1940 Crocker.

Al Crocker was a genius. This is one of his works of art.

A powerhouse for its day, with 60 hp out of 61 cubes.

The tension adjustment on the Crocker springer.

Quality workmanship abounds on any Crocker.

The engine-turned side case is a work of art.

Two Carb Bitsa

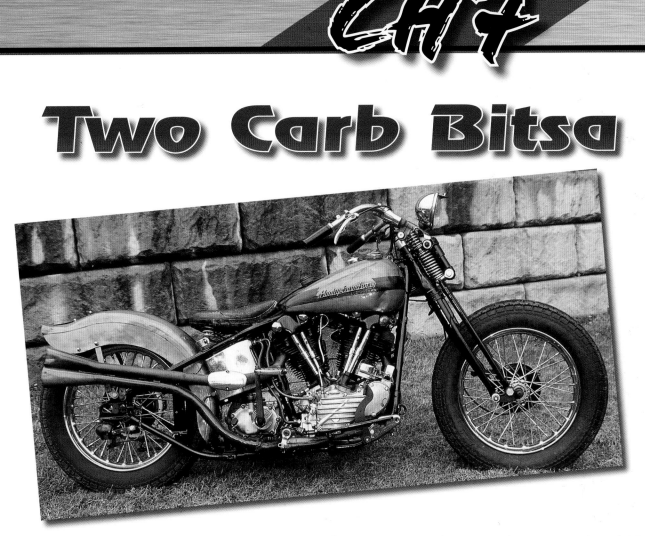

Guys who have been building and dealing in old motorcycles for many years wind up with extra parts – sometimes *lots* of extra parts. In some cases, there are enough parts to build another motorcycle. That's the case with Dale Walksler, and that's how this motorcycle came to be.

Dale calls this bike his 100th anniversary Harley. In 2003, while everyone else was celebrating Harley's 100 years with brand new motorcycles, Dale was taking parts from over Harley's many decades and making a vintage bike out of them.

This motorcycle is constructed completely out of used parts. There are no reproduction pieces here at all. He did all this in the course of 30 days. The man knows his Harleys. It would take most guys more than 30 days to figure out what goes together! And the parts still wouldn't *be* together.

Talented and experienced people like Dale can take *bitsa* this motorcycle and *bitsa* that one and make a fully functioning new motorcycle. Meanwhile, the rest of us are scratching our heads, wondering how he knew all that stuff would work together.

The foundation for this particular bike is a stock 1941 Harley-Davidson frame. To that was added a 1942 Harley XA front springer fork, chosen because it is 2-1/2 inches longer than a standard Harley springer.

See chapter 8 for more about Harley XAs, but suffice it to say, that average guy doesn't have XA forks lying around, OK?

For a bike made up of parts, this Two-Carb Special looks like a factory job.

Bitsas have special bits.

Early accessory pipes sing a sweet song

The heartbeat for this bike is a 1940s Knucklehead that Walksler built up out a pair of NOS cases. You read that right, New Old Stock.

To that, he added pieces and parts from his own personal parts stash, including stock cylinders and some fairly rare dual carb heads. Twin Linkert M35 carbs use a pair of 1930s dust covers (as opposed to actual air cleaners). At the other end of the combustion cycle, an old set of oval accessory pipes takes care of exhausting duty.

A stock four-speed transmission feeds the power to an 18-inch rear wheel. The front wheel is a matching size and the tires are vintage Goodrich. The brakes at both ends are 1930 Harley VL style.

The rest of the bike is just as much of a mixture as the engine. The dented Fat Bob tanks are complemented by an equally un-straight rear fender that started life as a 1936 Harley VLH *front* fender. The seat is a period accessory Bates model that is also showing its age.

The handlebars on this Twin Carb Parts Pile Special were once used by four-time *consecutive* (1958 through 1961) AMA Grand National Champion Carroll Resweber. The hand controls are vintage accessory Trigger Locks. The headlight is a King Bee Model 98-99. Taillights are a pair of old bullets.

For the finish on the sheetmetal, Dale opted to media blast the parts and then coat them with

Dale Walksler has an eye for what looks right for any period H-D.

GM's Delco Remy Division supplied electrical components.

King Bees have lit the way for decades.

Springer is from a 1942 XA, 2 ½-inches longer than a standard Harley.

original 1930s Harley-Davidson clear shellac. It gives the sheetmetal a bit of an aged patina look, which is most fitting. The metal is 70 years old and so is the "paint."

Like nearly all Dale Walksler-built and tuned bikes, this one starts on the first or second kick and goes like stink. It's tradition.

When Johnny Came Marching Home

Anyone over the age of 40 has heard the stories and seen the advertisements for military surplus Harley-Davidsons, still in the crate and packed in Cosmolene. Some of the stories are true; yet most are probably not. One thing is true, though. All Harley XAs were military surplus because the bikes were built *only* for the military.

During the early stages of World War II, the US Army was deeply involved in the North African theatre. The terrain there was like none the troops had experienced in motorized wartime.

The heat and the sand were deadly enemies of the WLA motorcycles the Army was using at the time. V-twin engines with the cylinder's situated parallel to the frame tend to run very hot, especially on the wind-blocked rear cylinder. Additionally, sand tends

Leonard Andres built this XA.

to wear out the chains and sprockets extremely quickly.

The Army leadership noticed that the German BMWs did not seem to be experiencing the same problems. Their horizontally opposed cylinders were sticking out in the cooling air, and their shaft drives were almost impervious to the sand.

The War Department commissioned Harley-Davidson and Indian to develop a motorcycle that would perform as well as the German's BMW. The specifications included shaft drive, horizontally opposed engines, and greater ground clearance.

The two companies' approaches were somewhat different. Indian built a shaft-driven, transverse 90-degree v-twin very similar in appearance to Moto Guzzi's future layout. The Indian was called the

Hard to believe a military bike could become so beautiful.

This XA has 1947 Harley instruments.

XA springers were two inches longer for better ground clearance.

Model 841. Harley-Davidson basically copied the BMW R-71. They dubbed the bike the XA.

Approximately 1,000 XA models were built, but none ever made it to Africa. The XAs were shipped to Camp Holabird (Maryland), Fort Knox (Kentucky) and Fort Carson (Colorado) for evaluation purposes. By the time the evaluation period was finished, the African part of the war was dying down.

That fact and the introduction of the Jeep ended the H-D XA and Indian 841 project. The bikes never saw civilian production, though they met the Army's needs very well. So did the Jeep, though, and the Army went the four-wheeled route instead.

The XA engine is a near copy of the BMW R71.

The first and only Harleys built with shaft drive.

1947 FL fenders and straight pipes adorn the XA that Andres built.

After WWII, the U.S. government disposed of the XAs and their spare parts as military surplus through their normal surplus sales channels. They wound up in civilian hands after all and some Harley experts believe that as many as 500 of the bikes may still be in existence.

That's a pretty good percentage by anyone's count, especially considering the government rigors that they survived. That two of the XA models wound up in the same place is amazing, considering the 60-plus years that have passed and the fact that they both took different routes to wind up in their new home with Dale Walksler and his Wheels through Time Museum.

Dale found the white bike very near its original home, Ft. Knox. Dale states the bike was put into civilian trim in the late 1940s and has not been changed since then. He likes to keep his bikes in "as found" condition whenever practicable in order to allow them to retain as much of their history as possible. According to its serial number, this bike is the seventh XA built.

Like all XAs, it has a 750 cc (45-cid) horizontally opposed twin engine, rear suspension, and shaft drive. It is the more original and stock-equipped of these two.

At this late date, it is unknown who actually converted the bike from military to civilian trim, but it is a well-preserved example of what likely happened to many of the original XA models.

The purple XA here has a bit better known history and has been touched by legendary hands. AMA Hall of Famer Leonard Andres gets credit for the build of this one.

Andres was a successful Harley-Davidson dealer in California following his equally successful professional racing career. Leonard was a tuner extraordinaire, building seven Daytona 200 winning engines.

The white XA has been kept in "as found" condition.

He was also the builder/tuner for his famous son, Brad. Brad Andres holds the distinction of being the only rider in AMA history to win his first and last professional Grand National races. He was also the only one to ever win the Grand National Championship in his rookie season. He was kinda good.

This XA bobber is extremely well-finished, as one would expect from a bike out of Leonard Andres' shop. It wears the dealership sticker from his original Modesto location, though he later had dealerships in San Diego and Sacramento, too.

The bike has had some updates, too. Those include 1947 Harley FL fenders and a 1947 seat, too. The instruments are from 1947 as well. Hmm, there seems to be a pattern here. The most obvious change to the purple bike is the addition of Borrani rims.

Both of these bikes run great but sound different. Their pipes are different for one thing. The white XA has stock style mufflers, while the purple one has long straight pipes. That one has also had the magic hands of Leonard Andres on the engine. All engines should be so lucky.

No not James Bond; this "007" refers to the serial number...

Stock style mufflers are used on this one.

The original lubrication/ service tag still is in place.

The white XA is all original from it's early civilian days.

Originally most XAs had blackout headlights.

The front end was crafted by Ventura Motorworks.

Daily Rider Indian Bobber

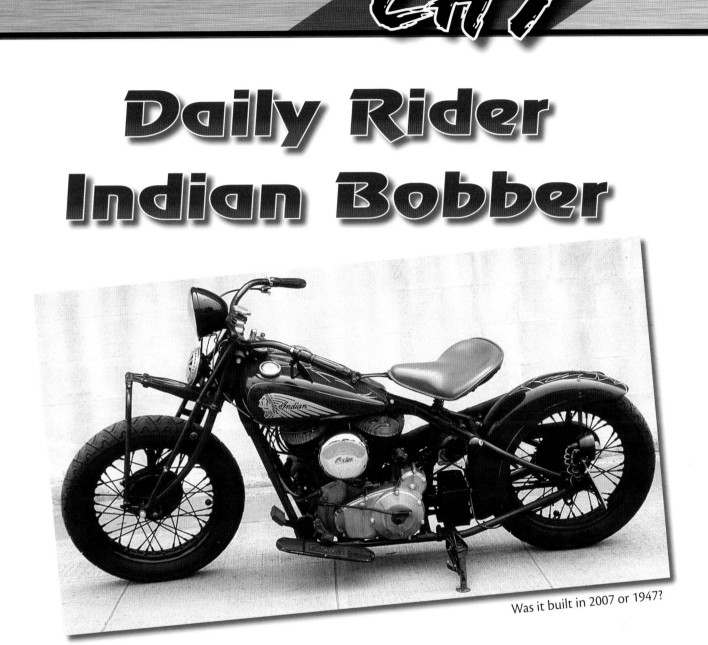

Was it built in 2007 or 1947?

Early bobbers were often the owner's only mode of transport, so they were often ridden daily – back and forth to work or school. No reason that cannot still be the case, is there? Nope. Not if the bike is dependable and fits the rider, like this 1936/46 Indian belonging to Joe Moody.

Joe's Indian was constructed by the extremely talented and meticulous Kurt Morrow at Ventura Motorworks, Ventura, California. Kurt is of the

opinion that motorcycles are meant to be ridden and ridden often.

When he builds a bike, it runs like a new one, even if it's based on 60- or 70-year-old components. Truth is, Kurt's contraptions run better than a lot of newer bikes, including ones costing twice as much and running brand new engines.

Kurt says this Indian "looks like a stock Chief that's been cut down, but it's really a very custom

Joe Moody did the paint on his bike.

Belt-driven alternator is the only clue to updates.

Deflectors keep exhaust off the paint.

The Autolite distributor still does yeoman's duty.

Crocker steering damper keeps the front end tight.

It's real.

Who wouldn't want to ride this beauty every day?

Chief made to fit Joe like he built it himself. This bike is ridden every day around Ventura."

The frame for this build is a vintage 1936 Indian and has 28 degrees of rake. Into that 70–plus-year-old frame, Kurt bolted a 1946 Indian Chief 74-cubic-inch engine. Of course, he worked the engine over pretty well first, Ventura Motorworks style.

That means Kurt measured and inspected every piece that went into it, improving bearing surfaces, blueprinting tolerances and so forth. Basically he took Indian engine and transmission technology and moved it into the 21st century, since the guys from Springfield couldn't do it themselves.

The carburetor is a Linkert and it's covered by a Ventura Motorworks custom air cleaner. Exhaust pipes are VM customs, too.

The front end is another custom unit made by VM, a recurring theme on this bike. It looks exactly

right on the '36 frame. The gas tank is a modified Chief unit, while the handlebars and controls are custom by… you guessed it, VM.

Kurt modified the Indian foot controls. The front fender became the rear fender. The Duolamp taillight is on a custom mount. Brakes are custom by… well, you know.

The thing about Kurt's work is that he doesn't call attention to it on the bike.

Only an Indian purist would recognize the fact that many of the stock-looking components are not really stock at all. They are either new parts or modified Indian parts. Many who see Kurt's work think he is a restorer rather than a custom bike builder. That's about the biggest compliment anyone can pay him, Kurt believes.

The Squarester

What in the world is this thing? Is it a chopper? Is it a bobber? Is it a special? Is it a…?

Doug Wothke of Huntsville, Alabama, owns the bike in question. At various times he has referred to it as either the "Squarester" or the "Four-ster." In actuality, it is a combination of an Ariel Square Four engine and a 1952 Harley K-Model chassis.

"The bike was built in the early '60s from a wrecked Ariel Square Four and a blown-up Harley K-Model," explains Doug. "Unfortunately, the builder was dead when I found the bike, so I don't know much more about it. It's really well made and the modifications look so nice, you'd think it was a factory-made bike. It runs good and is a lot of fun to ride. Also confuses the hell out of most people."

Ariel Square Fours are among the most collectible of British motorcycles. The engine in this hybrid is out of a 1956 model, produced just two years before the last ones in 1958. As such, it has most of the improvements that Ariel made over the two decades they built Square Fours.

Doug has ridden the bike quite a bit and states that it's an easy starter and performs very well.

The Harley K-Model was introduced in 1952 and became the predecessor of the later Sportster. The fact that this particular bike's chassis is from that first

The original owner did an excellent conversion.

The best of both worlds – Harley and Ariel.

In an earlier iteration, the Squarester's sheetmetal must have been blue.

year of production causes some consternation among antique Harley-Davidson restorers. That doesn't bother Doug any.

He's been known to cause a little gnashing of teeth over the years anyway.

In Doug's defense, though, he didn't build the bike. The original owner built it at a time when neither donor bike was considered as desirable nor as collectable as they are today. In reality, he saved both of them.

How many wrecked motorcycles' engines have turned to rusted, locked-up lumps over the years because no one did anything with them? By the same token, how many engine-less chassis have sat outside behind barns and garages until they deteriorated to worthlessness? Many thousands of both.

That fate didn't befall either half of this bike. Thank goodness (and an enterprising builder) for that.

The distinctive lump – a 1956 Ariel Square Four.

The Ariel Engine is British, from 1956.

Conversion to Squarester was accompanied by some custom paint.

The componentry was installed neatly.

The Burman four-speed transmission is a sought-after item.

The fender has been bobbed – it must be a bobber!

Four straight pipes sing a sweet song.

The seat is wide and comfy, even on all-day rides.

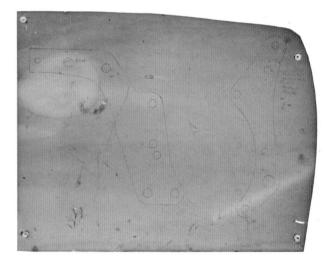

The original owner's cardboard motor mount template.

All business, the Mills' Indian is lean.

Josh Mills' Indian

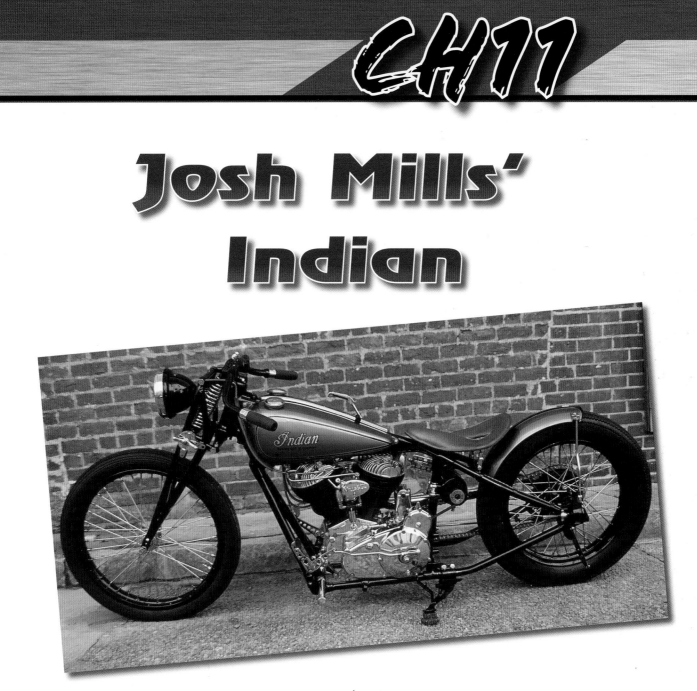

Josh Mills is a talented hot rodder, as well as a skilled motorcycle builder. He owns his own fabrication business, Mills & Company, in Marietta, Georgia.

He basically started with a pile of somewhat related parts and an idea. Oh, yeah, and a bunch of talent.

The talent was probably the most important ingredient. Without that, it would still be a pile of parts-like most people's projects!

Josh was willing to step into foreign waters with the build of this bike. He had little knowledge of Indians and their parts interchangeability when he started the project.

"I didn't know the first thing about what I was looking at as far as what was available or rare as hen's teeth and how it fit together."

Hey, there's nothing like learning on a project with a specific deadline, right?

Built in 2005, Mills' Indian has the look of a classic board-track racer.

The '47 Indian Chief engine was built by Mike McMullen.

The 21-inch front wheel has no brake. The tire is an Avon.

Deadline? Yes, this bike was one of the entrants in *The Horse Backstreet Choppers* magazine's 2005 Chop-Off. That is an annual event in conjunction the magazine's "Smoky Mountain Smoke Out" in Salisbury, North Carolina.

The beginnings of the bike you see here were not as pretty a sight. Basically what Josh had in hand was a partial basket case made up of parts from various years. The 74-cubic-inch engine is from a 1947 Chief, while the frame is a 1933 rigid. You get the idea.

As with most basket cases, even the parts he did have needed repair or some tweaking. Make a mental note – that's why they wind up in baskets.

The engine had some broken fins and a damaged mount. The frame had some cracks in the neck that required a little corrective surgery. What can you expect for motorcycle parts that are 50- to 60-plus years old? If it were easy, anyone could do it!

Josh found some Indian experts to help him with the intricacies and idiosyncrasies of Indians. One was a local, Mike McMullen. Mike's brain was picked

Not much wind resistance here!

The rear brake was sourced from The Shop in Ventura, CA.

on a regular basis. Another invaluable source of knowledge (and parts) turned out to be Kiwi Indian in California.

Mike Thomas at Kiwi knows his stuff, too, just like the other Mike. Between the two of those experts and with Josh's own work, they came up with all the necessary Indian bits to make the 74-cubic-inch twin purr.

McMullen did the rebuild and incorporated Kibblewhite valves and stock milled heads. Cams are stock, too, and the carburetor is a Linkert M-BONN. The air cleaner came from Chopper Dave's Casting Company. Ignition is from a Morris magneto. McMullen built the transmission, too. The shifter is from a 1939 Ford.

It's a Chief engine from 1947 with a Linkert carb.

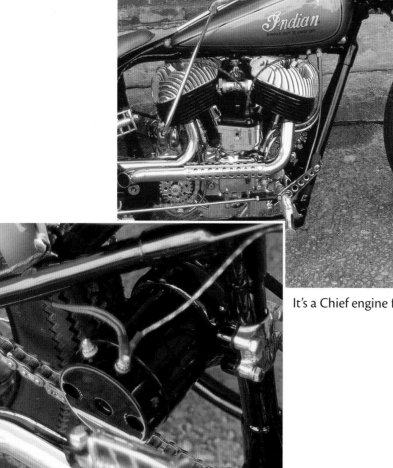

The Cycle Electric generator is belt-driven.

Josh says, "The cases were modified by cutting the original magneto mount off the front, as well as the front half of the cam cover. To do this I had to re-route the breather from the front of the motor, through the oil pump and through the can cover."

The fuel tank and oil tank have some subtle changes in the form of being narrowed by 1-3/4 inches each. The beautiful blue paint was applied by Terry Southern. Atlanta area master Bill Abrams applied the striping and Indian lettering. The custom trim on top of the tanks is from a 1940 Ford hood.

One of the common practices these days in rear fender acquisition is to cut a ribbed 1930s automobile spare tire cover and make a couple of fenders out of it. That's what Josh did. His cover was from a '35 Chevy. The headlight is a vintage one, an Old Sol. The taillight is a WWII surplus unit.

The front end on the Indian is a girder from a 1941 Scout. It required a longer neck stem to fit the 1933 frame.

All the bikes in the Horse Smoke Out Chop Off are always outstanding bikes, each one good enough to win a normal bike show. But this wasn't a normal bike show and there could only be one winner out of the four outstanding contestants.

The final vote count revealed Josh Mills' Indian as the winner. Gaze at the pictures and see why.

Mike McMullen stitched the leather on the Mills seat pan.

The Old Sol headlight is a rare vintage component.

The Mills & Company logo.

Ventura Highway Pan/Shovel

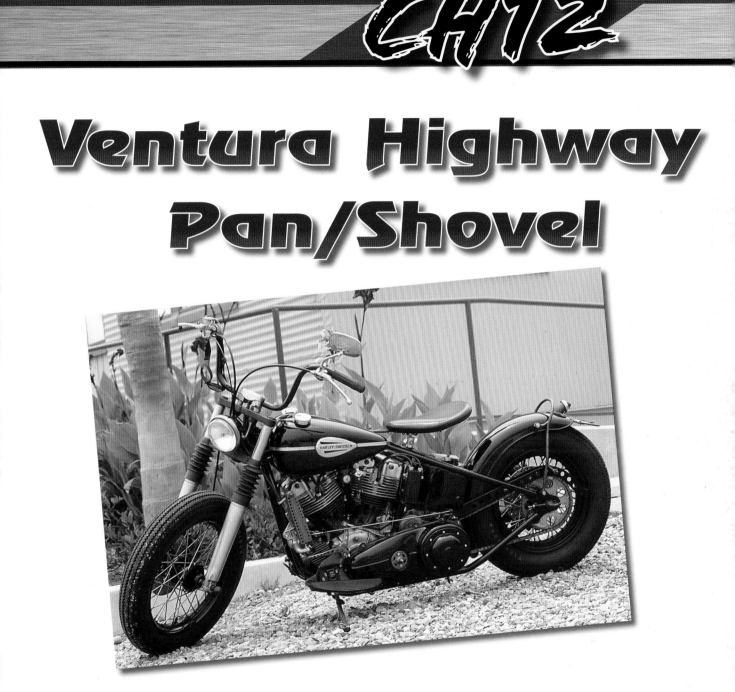

Ventura, California, is getting a bit of a reputation for some very sweet vintage choppers and bobbers that reside there. This black Pan/Shovel is typical of the reason for that notoriety. Although its owner, Jeff Ando, resides in nearby Santa Barbara, the bike is pure Ventura Motorworks.

Kurt Morrow is the man behind VM and he has an uncanny eye for the exactly correct look for a Harley

bobber. He also has the talent and skill to pull it off. Before you stands an excellent example of that truth.

The nucleus for this bike was a 1963 Harley Panhead engine. Kurt rebuilt and modified the 74-cubic-inch Panhead lower end and added a 1966 Shovelhead's better breathing heads.

It's a common combination, but Kurt's expertise makes it a trouble-free, first-kick-starting

Kurt Morrow knows the right proportions.

Panhead bottom, Shovelhead heads makes a good combo.

The modified Fat Bob tanks.

Kick me.

It's a Paughco rigid frame slightly modified.

This primary cover hides a VM belt drive.

masterpiece. The engine feeds power through a belt primary drive to a modified (read smoothed-out) Harley 4-speed transmission.

The carburetor is a modified (of course) S&S Super E breathing through a custom Ventura Motorworks air cleaner. Yes, the primary cover is a custom one, too. Should have known.

The frame for this bike is a modified Paughco rigid. Paughco has been building top-quality chopper and bobber frames for more than 30 years.

Paughco is a standard in the industry and Kurt uses their frames quite often if a suitable stock Harley frame is not available. There is no stretch, either in the backbone or downtube. This is a bobber, remember?

To the Paughco frame were fastened modified Harley Fat Bob gas tanks. The rear fender is a customized Indian Chief piece. No front fender. The headlight, taillight, foot and hand controls, and handlebars all received the Ventura Motorworks custom treatment. So did the seat.

On modern California roads with wall-to-wall traffic, brakes are an important feature and one that Kurt Morrow gives much attention.

The VM custom seat is wide and comfortable.

Foot controls are by Ventura Motorworks.

Custom pipes sing a pretty lullaby.

Try to imagine a better looking bobber – can't do it.

Tires are vintage style Firestones.

Craftsmanship is *not* a lost art.

The VM custom taillight has a taste of Sparto.

Even the master cylinder has the right period look.

Jeff has the security of Ventura Motorworks' specially-built four-piston disc brakes at both ends of his bike. They stop the bike with authority, yet do not detract from the overall look of the bike. After all, the impetus behind building a bobber in the first place is enhanced performance over a stock motorcycle. That includes braking performance.

It's difficult to beat a pretty gloss black paint job enhanced with a few shiny baubles. Bill Kee at Vintage Restorations applied the flawless black coat, completing and complementing the handiwork. It's a gorgeous ride.

Front forks are Harley "Narrow Glide" for good handling.

CH13

Frankenstein Pan/Evo

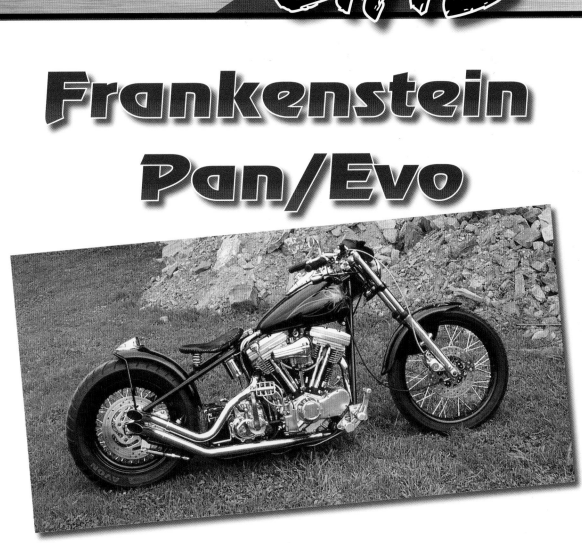

A motorcycle doesn't have to be old to exhibit some old school style. A perfect example of that is Konrad and Melinda Thiele's Pan/Evo-powered bobber.

Konrad built his bike the old school way. He gathered the parts one at a time from several different sources until he had all the components to build the bike. He took the concept a little further than most in that aspect though. His part-gathering escapades took place on two continents!

Konrad is a native of Germany, but he's always been a fan of American motorcycles,

especially Harley-Davidsons. So when he scoured the swap meets in and around his former homeland, he was looking in the H-D boxes, not the ones for BMWs or Zundapps.

When he came to the United States to live a few years ago, he brought his stash of parts with him. In his newfound home, he continued the parts search. The assembled result of his search efforts is one of the coolest little bobbers you'll ever come across. For obvious reasons, the bike is named Frankenstein.

Nashville, Tennessee, is home to this green and black beauty. Whenever Konrad and

As viewers approach Konrad's bobber, eyes start rushing all over the details.

Vintage-style Harley cat's-eye instrument cluster.

The tail lamp is best viewed from above!

Melinda take their portable TNT Performance Dyno dynamometer to motorcycle rallies and swap meets these days, they take Frankenstein along for the ride. The bike is always a hit. It is one of those bikes that everyone likes and it's not uncommon to see other bikers down on their hands and knees inspecting the handiwork.

Frankenstein's frame is a Santee rigid utilizing stock rake and no stretch. The front end is a Harley "Narrow Glide" piece, which assures good handling characteristics. Flanders handlebars are fitted with 1976 Harley hand controls. There's a cat's eye style instrument pod atop the Harley Fat-Bob tanks. The leather seat was acquired at one of those European swap meets, specifically one in Norway. The taillight is another swap meet find.

It's in the 96-cubic-inch power plant that this bike really earns its moniker. The engine

Check out the hard-plumbed copper oil lines.

Shiny stuff of several colors works great together on this bike.

is mostly an aftermarket amalgam of Harley Panhead-style parts mixed with Evo-style pieces to make it breathe better. It's a healthy combo.

The cases and heads are from STD, but the cylinders came from Axtell. The ignition is a tried and true Crane points-style. The carburetor is the ubiquitous S&S G. The air cleaner came from "Eric's swap box," according to Konrad. Konrad formed the custom exhaust pipes by hand. The transmission is mostly a 1979 model, but with a 1969 main shaft. Get the point?

The mile-deep black paint wears beautiful marbled green graphics and striping, all applied by Browder Ledbetter. Needless to say, Browder is renowned around the Middle Tennessee area for his painting skills.

Like any well-crafted vehicle, Frankenstein is more than just a combination of parts. It is Konrad's craftsmanship in the hand-formed pieces and assembly that sets the bike apart.

A case in point is the execution of the sweeping copper oil lines. Note that they are hard-plumbed at both ends. No rubber insurance fittings here, folks! It's that type of detail that brings Konrad's fellow bike builders to their knees…literally.

High performance Axtell cylinders are near bulletproof.

The leather seat was located at a swap meet...in Norway!

The belt drive and chromed details stand out.

This Frankenstein combines beauty with beast.

Black and green paint is the handiwork of Browder Ledbetter.

Even the headlight wears the Ledbetter green marble.

Tail lamp is a swap meet item of unknown origin.

The fork is a modified Wide Glide.

Greco's Shovel Bobber

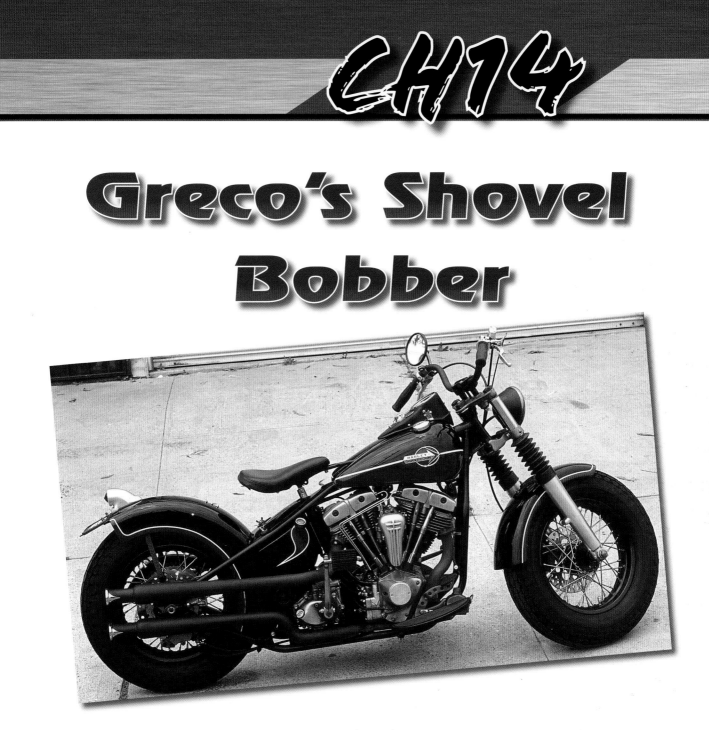

Shovelheads make great bobbers. Of all the Harley engines, the Shovelhead combines a vintage appearance with fairly modern Harley internals. Aftermarket and OEM parts are relatively easy to come by for Shovels, too. It's a bit of the best of both worlds.

Mike Greco's Shovelhead engine uses a mixture of the best components of those two sources of parts. Now displacing 86-cubic-inches instead of the original 80, his 1976 model shares a combination of Harley cases and S&S lower end internals.

The cams are S&S, as are the pistons. The ignition utilizes points, just like in the old days. The carburetor is an S&S Super E. The engine was assembled and balanced by Kurt Morrow at Ventura Motorworks. The pipes are custom, fashioned by Kurt. The air cleaner is by VM, too. The transmission is a stock '76 Harley 4-speed.

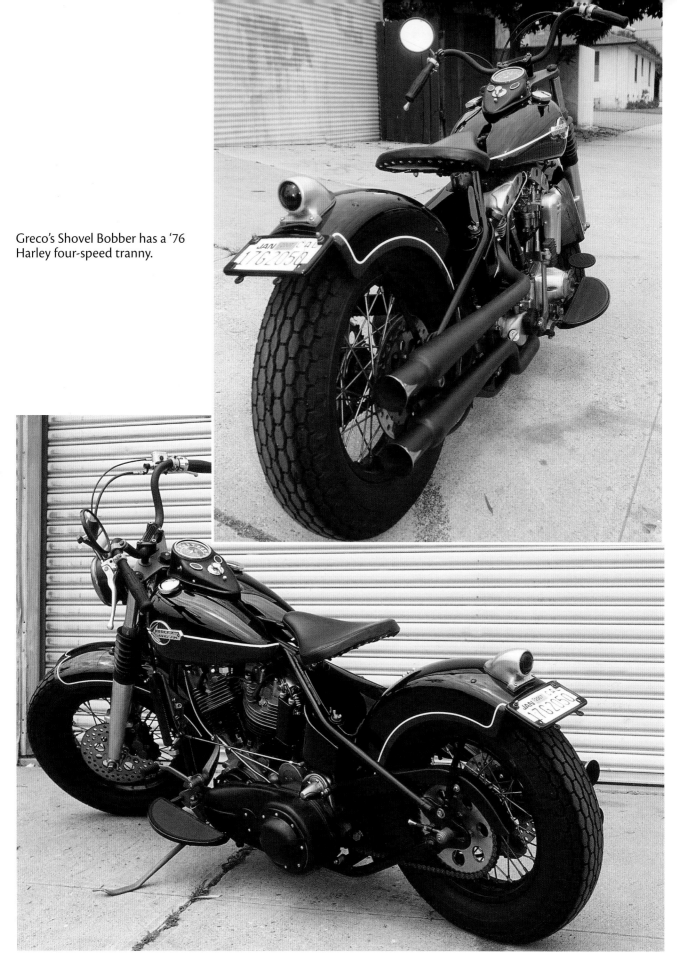

Greco's Shovel Bobber has a '76 Harley four-speed tranny.

Fenders, handlebars and more are by Ventura Motorworks.

The Sparto-style taillight got the VM treatment, too.

Custom pipes by VM

Bobbers have 'boards.'

Kurt calls Greco's motorcycle a "muscle bobber" because it has the traditional bobber look and style, but the reworked engine gives it some extra muscle.

The frame is a Paughco wishbone rigid with no additional stretch or rake. The tanks are modified Harley originals and the oil tank is a customized Harley Softail tank. Macs of Ventura created the seat. Kurt insists that bobbers are supposed to have footboards, not pegs, so that's exactly what this one wears.

Almost all the accessories were either created or modified by Ventura Motorworks. That list includes the headlight, taillight, fenders, handlebars, and risers. These guys can't leave well enough alone. Well, actually it's not "well enough" until Kurt has touched it a little bit.

The Wide Glide front forks got a little rework, too, naturally. "Whoa" is as important as "go" in Ventura County, so this bobber wears some handsome but powerful stoppers in the form of VM disc brakes with custom-hung four piston calipers. Sixteen-inch tires are by Coker Tire Company.

After the fabrication was completed, everything was pulled back apart and shipped off to Bill Kee at Vintage Restorations for the pretty PPG black and red paint.

A bike of the quality exhibited by Mike Greco's two-tone beauty does not come easily. Morrow says he has 300 hours invested in the building of this bike. Looking at the detail involved in it, that's not difficult to believe.

The VM air cleaner on the S&S Super E carb.

Two-tone paint is by Bill Kee.

Speedo and vital signs are raised for easier viewing.

Shovelheads have a vintage look, with fairly modern internals.

SECTION THREE:
CHOPPERS

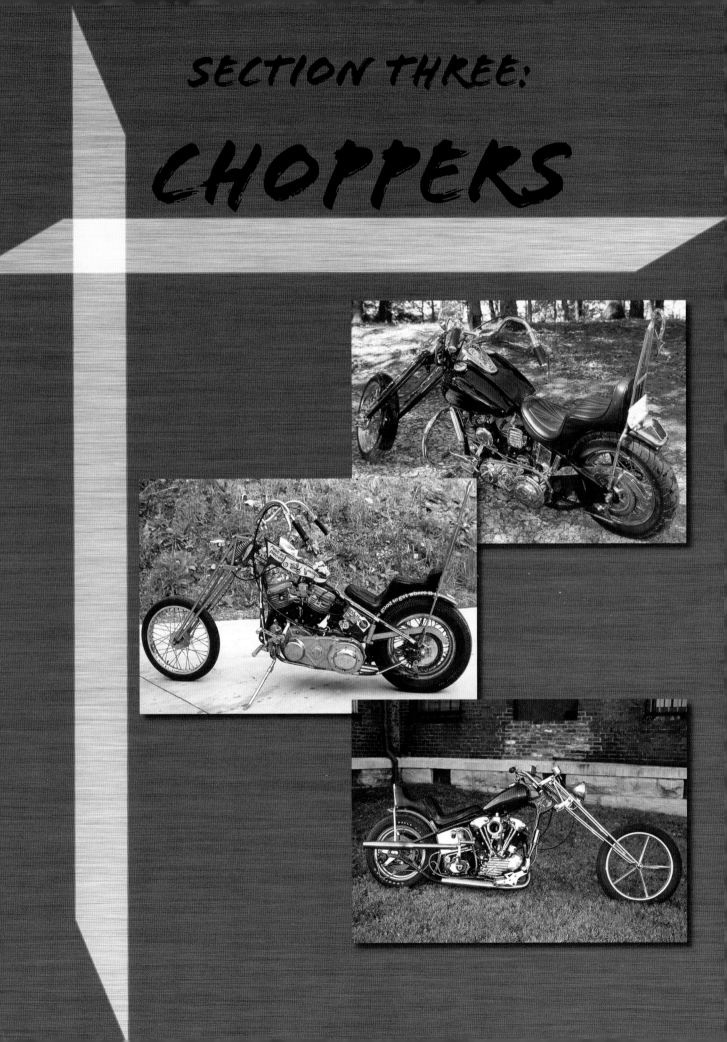

Stillman Small's Knucklehead Chopper

Knucks – some chopper guys insist that a Harley Knucklehead makes the best chopper, period; end of discussion. A few moments spent perusing Stillman Small's 1947 Knuck might have you agreeing.

The thing about a Knucklehead is that the engine just looks so mechanical. There was no attempt to hide anything. It has all kinds of shapes and ridges and bumps, a mechanical feast for the eyes. They run pretty good, too. They were in production from 1936 through 1947. This 1947 is the last of the breed and carries all the upgrades and improvements that H-D made over the years.

Stillman's Tennessee chopper is very much the type of bike that a guy might have built in the early 1970s, and then improved upon each year during

Paint is the handiwork of Wheels of Time.

the cold weather shutdown. The basics are 1947 Harley, but it has a few later upgrades to enhance performance and safety.

The most noticeable improvement would have to be the rear disc brake. That was a really wise move since there ain't no front brake! The vintage Invader wheels (19-inch front and 16-inch rear in this instance) have such a clean design that many chopper builders choose not to clutter the front one up with a brake.

That's a swingin' deal as long as you don't ever have to stop. With no front brake, the back one needs to be effective. A Japanese disc is as good as it gets.

The front end is a desirable Fury adjustable girder. Since the 1947 models pre-dated hydraulic rear suspensions by a couple of years, the 1947 straight leg rigid frame was a keeper for a sound chopper

 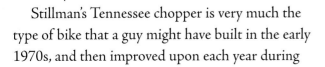

Chrome oil cooler adds to the longevity of the Knuck engine.

Only instrumentation is the Drag Specialties speedo.

Invader wheels are one of the better-styled chop items of all time.

Knuckleheads are all about the "knuckles" on top.

foundation. It was raked by just a little bit but not stretched.

The 1947 Knucklehead engine is mostly stock internally. It has been blessed with some Andrews cams and an SU carburetor sucking air through a big ol' horn velocity stack. Need to make things breathe and percolate correctly, you understand. Paughco built the pipes. Ignition is now 12 volt. In the interest of long engine life, an oil cooler has been mounted on the frame downtubes.

The original transmission is used but it has had a later ratchet lid installed.

Certain things make up a right-looking chopper. The lines of the various components have to complement each other for the bike to get the chopper-people-in-the-know seal of approval. Stillman's bike wears those pieces in the proper proportions.

Knucklehead breathes through SU carb and Paughco pipes.

King and queen seat has stash pouch on the side.

The molded neck wears battleaxe graphics.

Tank – the tried and true Mustang. Shaped right, not too big, not too small. Handlebars – Paughco T-bars. Just the right size and shape to let the simple controls fall readily to hand. Rear fender – five-inch flat. Front fender – uh, no.

The oil tank is from Paughco and the king and queen seat was custom made. Expensive parts don't always work any better than cheapies, so the headlight and taillight are of the latter persuasion, El Cheapo Incorporated.

Traditional choppers are as much about looking pretty as anything else, so this baby got some pretty paint in Candy Apple Red flavor. Wheels of Time Painting did the honors. Tasteful graphics include an airbrushed mural on the top of the tank and battleaxes on the molded frame neck.

Stillman's chopper is showing its age a little. That's because it has been ridden and not pampered. Seems that these days, the older they are, the more likely they are to be riders instead of polished dust collectors. Why is that?

Skeeter's Pan/Shovel

Skeeter Tipton's an old school chopper builder if there ever was one. He's been building choppers longer than most current chopper fans have been standing on two legs. He doesn't even *know* how many he's built.

What he does know, though, is that he likes Harley-Davidsons and he likes choppers. He also likes to mix components from different eras to build a bike that's mostly Harley, but that has the best of what he likes.

In the early years, The Motor Company made that easier than they do today. Fitting a Shovelhead top end to a Panhead lower is not a big deal. Lots of skilled engine guys, like Skeeter, do it all the time and create what we have here, a Pan-Shovel.

Skeeter built the springer himself.

The proprietor of Skeeter's Scooter Shop, Skeeter knows what components make for a strong, dependable engine, so his 1953-based mill got 'em. The cases are stock, but the cams are from Andrews. The Shovelheads are stock, but the pistons are by Wiseco. Originally having a displacement of 74-cubic-inches, Skeeter now describes it as being "80 inches plus."

The rest of the mechanical componentry on the engine includes a carburetor and air cleaner from S&S. Ignition is by points and the exhaust exits through simple drag pipes.

Gear changing duties are accomplished by a stock Harley ratchet shifter, vintage 1964.

Most choppers are in rigid frames. This one once carried a 1947 Harley Knucklehead engine. It has

Part Panhead, part Shovelhead—it's a Pan-Shovel!

been stretched two inches in the backbone. The rake is now 36 degrees.

Just like a lady's simple black dress is a staple, so is a simple black paint job on a chopper. Skeeter shot this one with Akzo Nobel's Sikkens premium. It's smooth as glass and looks a mile deep.

Old timey scooter builders like Skeeter are accustomed to doing some things themselves. That way they don't have to settle for what someone else's vision of the right part is. Case in point, the fenders on Skeeter's chopper. They are handmade. If you want something done right…

Ditto the front end. He built it himself at the shop and it's adjustable. On one end, you'll find a stock springer brake on a 19-inch laced wheel, accompanied by a Dunlop tire. At the other end,

Chain drive - simple, reliable and basic.

"Long ass springer" is the technical term.

six-bend bars sit atop six-inch risers. The rear wheel is the ubiquitous 16-inch Harley with a stock brake and Dunlop tire.

The headlight on this bike is the simple round sealed beam and the taillight is a tombstone style. A custom horseshoe oil tank with a remote filter keeps the oil clean. A stock Harley gas tank is used. The seat is a comfy custom, fit for a king and his queen. Dig that hand-formed sissy bar with the devil's tail curled on the end.

Skeeter's chopper is an example of what a real chopper should be in that it is built just the way he wants with no nod to current fads or trends. The crash bars are a nod to that standard. No one else is putting crash bars on choppers, so why does this bike have them? Because.

Crash bars are not a fashion statement; they're utilitarian.

The Pan/Shovel uses Andrews Cams and Wiseco Pistons.

There's a Harley gas tank plus a custom seat.

This paint finish is a shiny, deep black.

A visored 5¾-inch sealed beam headlight.

A textbook traditional chopper – Skeeter Tipton's Pan-Shovel.

A little dragon on the handmade front fender.

Springer is adjustable.

Skeeter's handmade devil's tail sissy bar.

Hard-to-beat tombstone taillight.

The front end is a combo of Durfee girder and Bates light.

Have a Coke and a Smile

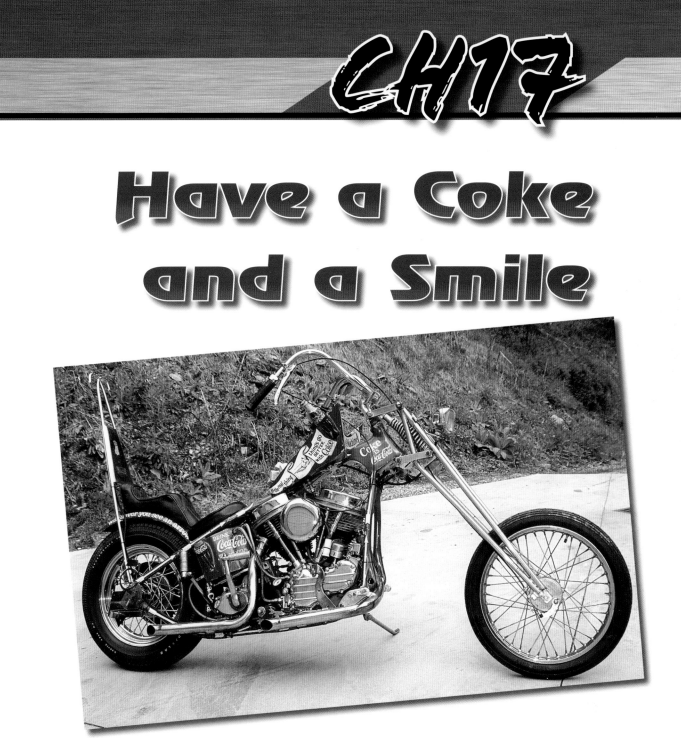

Theme bikes are nothing new. The viability of such has been debated over the years, even as it has been in recent years every time the crew at Orange County Choppers in New York screws one together. Hardcore bikers make fun of them, but the general public usually is drawn to them like a magnet.

For several decades, Coca-Cola paraphernalia has been an attraction for lots of people. There are some who collect every bit of Coca-Cola branded advertising piece that they can get their hands on. Some devote entire rooms of their homes as museums of the stuff. There are those who have even carried the theme to the extent of building a rare 1930s Cadillac convertible into a street rod with a Coca-Cola theme.

This "Coke Machine" Harley Panhead chopper is a result of that same fanaticism. Built in the early

The Coke theme is most apparent in the gas tank ice and bottle.

Various vintage Coca Cola themes are used.

1970s by Angela Johnston and David Cargill of Des Moines, Iowa, it is a rolling metal tribute to the storied red and white brand cola's marketing successes.

No other non-alcoholic beverage has ever inspired the passion that Coca-Cola has. We won't even try to speculate on why Coke has. Let's talk about the motorcycle.

The basis of the bike is a 1948 Harley-Davidson Panhead and in pretty much stock 74-cubic-inch configuration. The bike wasn't built just for show either. According to the back of the promotional postcard that Dale Walksler (Wheels Through Time Museum) supplied, the bike was drag raced and ran a quarter mile in 12.09 seconds at 120 mph.

That same postcard describes the chop as "a metal sculpture; a kinetic array of Coca-Cola nostalgia; a collage of advertising." It is definitely a collage of advertising, incorporating various catch phrases of

The frame neck is molded smooth.

Tried and true Panhead power for the "Coke Machine."

the custom king and queen seat, painted on the frame tubes, and formed into the sissy bar, as well as the speedometer mount hanging off the left side of the engine.

The fuel tank is a hand-formed, wing-shaped affair. At the back end of the tank, in the valley of the V, is a group of "ice cubes" with a Coke bottle rising out of it. The bottle theme also extends to the gas cap and the oil tank cap, where the cap is in the shape of the top half of the famous Coke bottle shape. Sometime in the past, the bottle top part of the oil tank cap has gotten lost, though.

Coke advertising from over the years. "The Pause that Refreshes" and "It's the Real Thing" are just a couple of them.

The "Coke Machine" also carries many reminders of Coca-Cola's "wherever you see an arrow" theme that began in the 1930s. That icon is stitched onto

Arrow theme is prevalent on the steel speedo mount.

Horseshoe tank has Coke bottle at filler and once had the entire bottle.

Hand-formed sissy bar carries out the arrow theme

Arrows are overlaid onto king and queen seat.

"Whenever you see an arrow..."

The more normal parts of the chopper follow standard late 1960s/early 1970s practices. The front end is the popular Durfee girder and the headlight is the rectangular-style Bates. The 21-inch front wheel utilizes a small Hallcraft's drum brake to supplement the stock Harley rear drum. Handlebars are pullbacks of unknown manufacture.

The rear fender is a five-inch flat style. There is no front fender on the bike these days, though the vintage postcard reveals there was one at one time in its early life.

Shortly after Johnston and Cargill built the "Coke Machine" they began to show it at various venues. The attitude toward choppers and their tie-in to established companies was a lot different in those pre-Discovery Channel days.

The Coca-Cola Corporation obtained what amounted to a cease-and-desist order forbidding the pair to advertise or show the motorcycle. It went into forced retirement for about 30 years. Finally, Dale Walksler acquired it...and Dale doesn't hide *anything*.

The weekend we spent in Maggie Valley, North Carolina, photographing the various bikes from Walksler's Wheels Through Time All-American Transportation Museum was also the first time Dale had started the "Coke Machine."

He put fresh gas in it, charged the battery for a couple of hours and kicked it about 10 times and it roared to life. The "Coke Machine" lives!

Mini front drum is from Hallcraft.

"The One" Thomas & Laura Groebel's 1980 Shovelhead

It's impossible to tell when this bike was built.

Basic black… and it's a fooler. Thomas & Laura Groebel's 1980 Shovelhead chopper is a fooler for sure.

At first glance, it doesn't catch your eye. Then you stand and look at it and you see the details. And then more details. Soon, you realize you can't take in *all* the details. The bike is just too, too *detailed*!

Kurt Morrow hasn't yet attained the oft thrown about title of "Master Builder." That's because whoever the self-proclaimed experts who bestow

Fat Bob tanks were axed and formed to this peaked beauty.

The front end is a shaved and modified Harley Glide.

Speedo is low to keep things clean.

that title on the latest TV star/bike builder are, they haven't seen Kurt's work. And they haven't seen him on TV either. That's because he's busy plugging away at Ventura Motorworks, his small shop on a Ventura, California, side street. He's cranking out some of the most gorgeous choppers and bobbers you'll ever lay eyes on, too.

Kurt is one of those few guys who have the eye for making a bike look exactly right. Exactly. He finds the right parts and makes the rest. Then he fashions them into functional, understated pieces of rolling art… the builder's art.

The Ventura Motorworks specialty is complete bikes. About all they farm out is the painting. Engine

The Shovel was rebuilt and balanced.

VMW pipes snake around controls.

Ventura chrome and Harley front from the rider's viewpoint.

builds are done in-house. So is machine work. And the machines are hand-cranked. No CNC production work here.

Everything is one-off, assuring the customers they won't see another bike like theirs at a run or show. Women don't like it with dresses at a dinner party and bikers don't like at a bike party.

This chopper started life as a 1980 Harley Davidson Shovelhead. The engine was completely gone through, rebuilt, and balanced by Kurt Morrow. It runs a stock points ignition and Andrews cams. The carburetor is an S&S Super E sucking wind through a Ventura MW air cleaner. The exhaust pipes are Ventura-created, too. Mufflers are the ever-popular (and deservedly so) cocktail shaker style.

To put the power from the healthy Shovel toward the rear wheel, a stock Harley transmission is used.

It's been enhanced, too. It's a custom polished, race-cut four-speed.

Everyone knows real choppers are hardtails these days, so a new Paughco straight leg frame was used. It has a 33-degree rake and is stretched two inches. It's painted gloss black as is the sheetmetal. The beautiful ebony PPG coats were applied by Bill Kee.

Macs of Ventura did the seat. It sits above a rear fender that once served as a front fender on a Harley Springer. It was flipped and modified for its new duty. Ventura Motorworks created the oil tank, the taillight, the pegs, the handlebars, and the risers. If you want it done right, gotta do it yourself.

The headlight is from a Ford Model A. The gas tanks were Fat Bobs, axed and welded and peaked. Look at the primary cover. Yep, it has a scoop on it.

The taillight mount is a VMW special.

The Ventura Motorworks touch - and logo - are evident.

Shovels make pretty chopper engines.

Stock-looking tin cover hides a belt drive.

The front brake is an enhanced Harley drum.

The headlight bracket is fashioned after a butt from Kurt's past.

That's to pull in a little cooling air to the *belt* primary that's hidden inside a relatively stock-looking tin.

The front end on a chopper is important to its look, as well as its handling. This one sports VMW-modified Harley forks, shaved. The front brake is a drum. Front wheel is a 21-inch laced one shod with an Avon Speedmaster tire.

The rear wheel is the standard 16-inch inside a Firestone tire. The brake is a disc with a VMW custom-hung four-piston caliper.

Attention to detail on this bike is outstanding. Even the ribbed brake pedal and foot pegs are custom-made Ventura Motorworks pieces. It's the complete package.

A custom-ribbed brake pedal matches the also-custom pegs and shifter.

CH19

Gennaro's Chicago Panhead

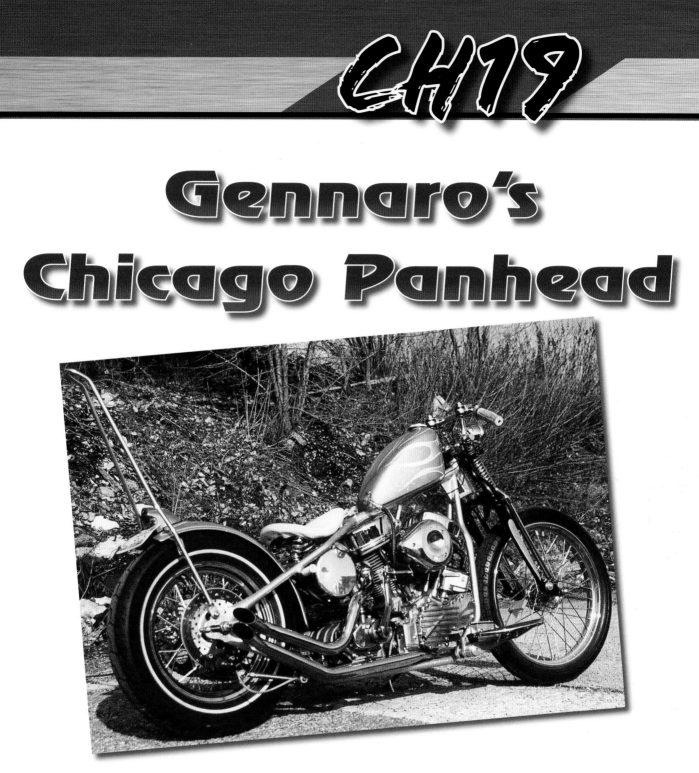

There's not much to say about Gennaro Sepe's '55 Harley Panhead other than it's just a pretty example of what to do right when building a chopper. It has "the look" that chopper builders seek and some never find.

Gennaro ought to know what a chopper is supposed to look and ride like. He's a feature editor for *The Horse Back Street Choppers* magazine. He sees many choppers up close and personal.

One of the corporate standards when seeking parts to build a correct chopper is Paughco. They have been supplying chopper builders with reasonably priced, high quality parts for decades.

Was it built in 1968 or today? It has the LOOK.

The short and sweet jockey shifter.

Paughco details add to the chopper look.

The white seat was an eBay find.

The oil filter keeps things clean inside.

Look, Ma, no brake!

That's where Gennaro headed when it came time to frame the foundation of his latest build.

The frame is a stock-specification wishbone style. He had to modify it a bit, of course. This is a chopper after all. Gennaro internally reinforced the backbone, shaved unneeded mounts and tabs, and window-paned the neck. While the Paughco catalog was open, a tall tilt-back sissy bar was checked off, too.

The engine started life as a 1955 Panhead. Gennaro wisely shipped it off to Weyland at Solutions Machining in Ft. Lauderdale, Florida. Weyland is well-known for his abilities with vintage Harley engines. He massaged the Pan into an 84-cubic-inch fire-breather utilizing an S&S stroker kit, S&S 585 cam and S&S Super E carburetor.

The heads are stock but they were treated to a high flow port job by Solutions. It's like a spa treatment for engines; it cleans things out and gets the juices flowing smoothly!

A Joe Hunt magneto lights the fire. Upswept pipes came from that great purveyor in the cosmos, eBay. The BDL foot clutch is complemented by a short jockey shift. Primary drive is via a two-inch belt. The transmission is from an early 1970s FX.

Voodoo Choppers in Detroit worked a little magic on the fuel tank, taking a 1970s XL piece and applying the Frisco treatment. When it, the rear fender and the frame were all prepped and ready for paint, Gennaro schlepped them all off to the guys who are becoming known as the Midwest

The neck of the Paughco frame got a little attention.

Flames on the gas tank hint at the fire-breathing engine below.

A flawless flake by Marty and Son.

The rear brake mount is by Fabricator Kevin.

Angled handlebars add to the look.

Metalflake Mavens, Marty & Sons in nearby Sycamore, Illinois.

Cars or motorcycles – it doesn't matter. Those guys are good! They used House of Kolor Spanish Lime Gold with pearl white and disco flake.

Flanders bars are a given on a traditional chop, but they gotta be chopped, too. These were drag bars that were shortened by a total of three inches off the ends and another three out of the middle. The result is a pair of lean bars that matches the equally lean motorcycle.

The front end is a 1948 offset springer replica. It got a little accent from the Metalflake magicians, too.

Risers are chrome-plated Flanders brass pieces. The headlight is a 4.5-inch version. The taillight is a Sparto.

There's only one brake, a back one by Fabricator Kevin. Wheels are star-hubbed Harley items. The seat came from the same famed supplier as the pipes, eBay. The ribbed oil filter housing is mounted low at the rear of the frame.

Gennaro had some building help from his pal Numnuts. They have succeeded in building a classic chopper, one that defies build dating. Was it built 40 years ago or was it built last year? If you can't tell, they did it right…in 2005.

The tall, forked sissy bar would be a good place for a sleeping bag.

CH20

Purple Haze

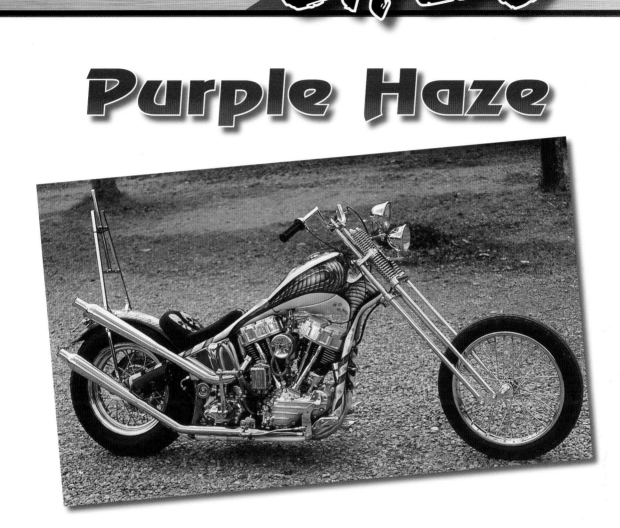

Jimi Hendrix was definitely out of it when he wrote *Purple Haze*, the song. Moe Saunders was right on the money when he built "Purple Haze," the chopper. The year was 1971 and this bike was perfect for the time.

Purple Haze was a show winner in the early 1970s and it's easy to see why. It has all the correct touches for the period and is wrapped in exquisite craftsmanship to boot.

After 33 years of riding and showing, and a few of neglect, the bike needed a refurbishment in 2004, so Moe redid it, but kept it in its original form.

Like all good Harley choppers of that early time, this one is powered by the preferred Harley-Davidson Panhead engine, a 1961 FL. Rebuilt by Moe, it features polished cases, finned cast heads and the stock 74-cube displacement with 8.5 to 1 compression ratio. The cams are 468 Siftons and the pipes are by Paughco (there's that name again). The bike runs a stock points-type ignition.

By the time Moe got around to rebuilding the engine on this bike in 2004, he had lived his share of kick-start motorcycles, so he converted this one to electric start. The kick starter is still operational,

Dale Walksler exercises his bikes often.

It's an 18-inch wheel without a brake on a classic springer.

The soft custom seat has a skull and chain motif.

Panhead engines look right in choppers.

The molded, ridged fuel tank is covered in white and purple pearl.

The paint and molding look great more than 35 years after application.

1971 and 2004 were the creation and refurb dates.

Kicker remains for those who like it that way.

though, and that is how current owner Dale Walksler starts the bike. He's a bit of a traditionalist, you know.

It's interesting to note that the paint on this baby is the original 1971 application. It has a few age checks in it and a couple of small chips, but otherwise it looks great. That is the mark of some excellent paintwork over a properly prepped motorcycle. From 25 feet, this looks like a new motorcycle.

The paint is a combination of purple over pearl white with a handsome stenciled graphic pattern and just a few starbursts. It's extremely well done and tasteful, especially by gaudy 1971 standards.

The fuel tank has some swirling ridges molded into it and in turn, it is molded into the frame. The raked and stretched 1955 Harley rigid frame itself has its own smoothly flowing molding. Again, extremely well done.

The front end is a springer of unknown manufacture. It is topped by Z-bars on custom risers. No front fender sits atop the Goodyear-shod 18-inch wheel that has no front brake. It was all the fashion to put twin-stacked headlights on choppers in the early 1970s. Sometimes they were rectangular, sometimes triangular. These are round ones.

The rear fender is a custom ribbed affair and it is topped off with a Bates-style taillight that has been molded into the fender. It sits over a 16-inch rear wheel with an Avon tire and a stock Harley brake.

Moe Saunders passed away in 2005. When he did, his family gave the bike to Dale Walksler for the Wheels Through Time Museum. They knew it would be appreciated and properly cared for, and they were right. It gets a great deal of attention there and gets ridden once in awhile, too.

Thin was in back in 1972.

Time Capsule Chopper

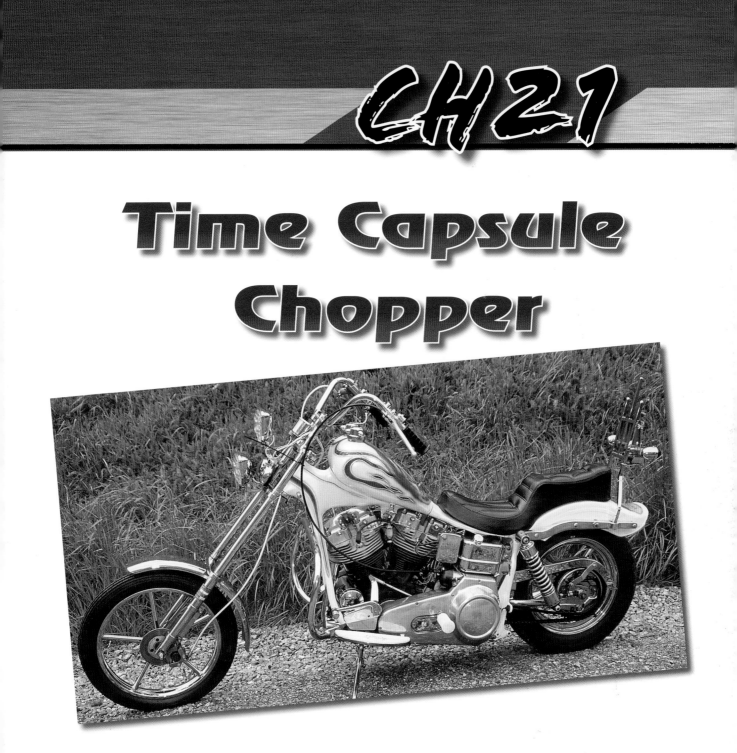

This 1970s-style chopper was *really* built in 1972…and 2000. It has been ridden a total of seven miles since completion. Yes, seven.

It's based on a 1968 Harley Davidson Shovelhead and its construction was started in 1972 by Bob (Smitty) Schmitt. Smitty's chosen theme for the bike was "narrow and low," according to his son Max. Max explained that the reason for the long, drawn-out build time was Smitty's health.

Smitty was a huge fan of the choppers he saw featured in various biker magazines in the late sixties and early seventies. He decided that he would like to have one for himself and set about carefully planning exactly what he would build. He gathered the necessary components and began building his dream bike.

Not long after Bob started building the chopper, though, he was diagnosed with cancer. When he

The custom front end is 5-inches over stock.

It has a Panhead lower and Shovelhead upper.

felt well enough he continued to chip away at the building of his chop.

Unfortunately, his illness worked faster than he could and he passed away before the bike could be completed. It sat in the family's garage for several years, as the family couldn't bear to part with it.

When Smitty had been building the bike, adult son Max was often by his side and he and Dad often kicked around the plans for the bike. Finally, Max decided it was time to finish building Bob's dream chopper. Ninety percent of the work was done already so Max just wrapped things up following Smitty's plans to the letter.

This bike is a great one to study as an example of what equipment and styling cues choppers had in 1972, because that's really what it is-a 1972 chopper. Heavily molded frames were the hot ticket on show-worthy choppers of the era and this one's hand-laid fiberglass frame molding has stood the test of time. It is still solid. The many coats of paint are starting to check just a little, but not enough to warrant any repair efforts.

The bike wears a paint job performed by one of Bob Schmitt's former coworkers and is signed simply "Duane." No one in the family can remember his last name. It was patterned after an early Frank Frazetta painting.

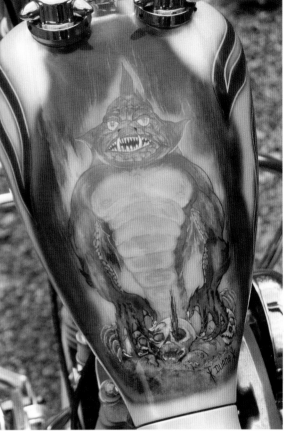

It's a 1969 Harley Pan/ Shovel Engine.

The Frazetta theme carries to the rear fender.

Duane – just Duane – painted the Frazetta-like monster.

The engine on the bike is a period-correct 1969 Harley Pan/Shovel (Panhead lower end, Shovelhead top end). It is stock and required no rebuild. Remember, it was only three years old when this bike's build commenced. It runs a Bendix carb.

The styling touches on the bike are from a day in time. The triangular Aris lights were *the* coolest lights available then. White grips and floorboards were just as trendy. Smitty hand formed the sissy bar and then he had it chrome plated at Brown's Plating. The custom front fork with concealed springs was extended by five inches. Dog bone risers and pullback handlebars are a given.

The seat on this bike is the ubiquitous 1970s Corbin Gentry stepped "king and queen." The king fared better than the queen on those seats. The gas tank and exhaust pipes were both made by Paughco, an early chopper parts supplier that has survived to this day.

Foot controls are the stockers. The front brake is a small Hallcraft hydraulic disc with a Borg Warner/ Spring Brummer master cylinder.

One of the main period touches is the round spoke chrome Invader wheels. Those were popular then and are highly sought after today. The round spoke ones are fairly rare as the diamond spoke

The Paughco tanks were fairly new when this bike was started.

The very rare B-W Spring Brummer master cylinder.

Twin Aris triangular lights – the hot setup.

Stock style floorboards are in white rubber.

Round spoke Invader wheels are highly sought now.

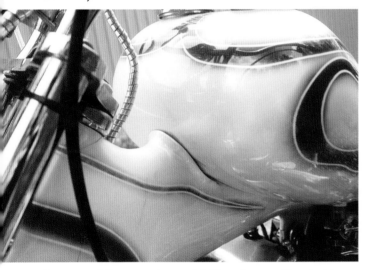

Frame molding was done with fiberglass and has held up very well.

Fork stops are commercial toilet handles.

models were most popular originally. Another interesting touch is the external fork stops. Look familiar? They're commercial toilet flush handles.

For some unknown reason, Smitty's dying wish to his family was that no one ride the bike. Max did renege on that promise on Father's Day 2001. That's when he put on the seven miles.

Since they'd promised not to ride the bike, and they didn't want Dad's pride and joy in the hands of some stranger, the family had to decide what to do with it. Their solution was to donate it to the Wheels Through Time Museum, where they knew that under curator Dale Walksler's watchful eye it would be preserved and cared for.

That's where it resides today, on the second floor mezzanine. It gives those of us who are students of chopper history a perfectly preserved example from 35 years ago.

It's significant in that unlike most of today's customs that are called "choppers" it has rear suspension. That's because this bike was actually chopped from a stock Harley Davidson. It's a *real* old school chopper.

Hackasaw's 45 Chopper

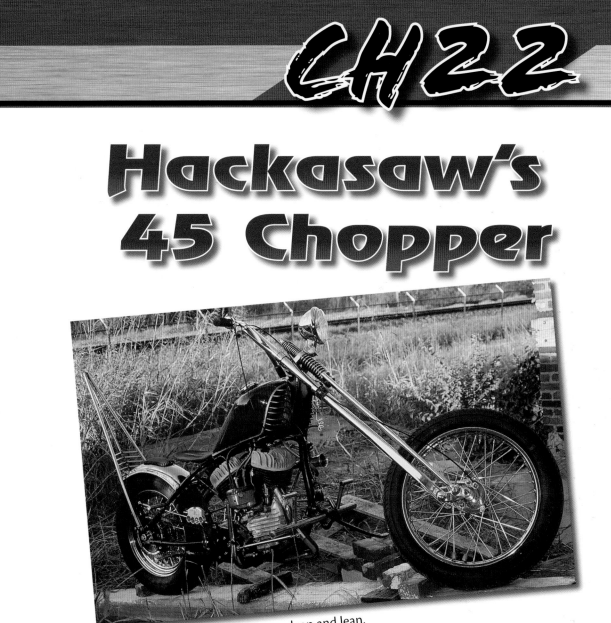

This is what choppers are about – clean and lean.

In these days of customs that look like a hundred other bikes, it's refreshing to come across the ones that are truly unique. Jerry "Hackasaw" Thigpen's Harley 45 is just that. It is an unusual combination of Harley parts, some British bits and a bunch of handmade, one-off pieces.

Hackasaw owns a small custom fabrication and parts shop (Visionary Customs) in the unlikely small town of Hartsville, Tennessee. He's been collecting, selling, and trading motorcycles and pieces of motorcycles most of his life. Every once in awhile, he'll take a pile of those

parts and form them into a motorcycle. Far from a purist, his mantra could be: "If it fits, use it. If it doesn't fit, let's make it fit. If it doesn't exist, let's make one."

This particular bike has a slightly overbored 1963 Harley 45 flathead engine, but it's running a rare Amal Concentric carb without the usual "tickler." That Amal is mounted facing forward on a custom stainless steel intake runner that Hack says functions as an adiabatic supercharger. Yes, that's a real word!

In nice weather he runs a velocity stack, but a K&N cone filter will fit right on that stack for

This chopper is part Harley, British and leftovers.

Custom risers and custom handlebars sit above a clean Paughco springer.

Notice the cold condensation on the intake runner. This was on a hot day.

monsoon conditions. Mark Hudson was the instigator of the unusual carburetor setup.

On a hot, but dry, mid-summer Tennessee day, we witnessed the effects of that long intake runner on the front-and-center Amal. After just a short ride, it became cold to the touch and was sweating like a glass of iced tea on a hot day.

The frame is a "1941-ish" Harley 45 frame and the three-speed transmission was made in 1946. Jerry also made the stout, stainless forward controls working the brake and suicide clutch. The jockey shifter is a hand-fabricated, bolt-on affair.

That fuel tank is made up of the pieces of two Honda tanks, combined with pieces of Harley and British oil tanks. The left section and right rear of the tank hold fuel, while the right front section contains oil and has a glass return tube visible from the rider's

seat. The interiors of both tank sections are lined with a heat and solvent resistant Mil Spec material.

The grille work on the tank's front is stainless. Welding is by TIG. Mr. Sins smoothed out the rough spots on the tank. John Snider painted it. The fuel tap is from some unidentified crotch rocket.

The rear fender started life as another British piece. It's stainless, too, and has been massaged to fit properly in its new home. The seat is another unique component. It was custom built and sits atop a dual air chamber and a hydraulic shock. It was covered in brown leather. The cursory pillion pad matches.

Lighting comes from a couple of vintage lamps. The rear is an old Wipac unit that is mounted on a titanium bracket. The front is from unknown origin. It sits on a 12-inch over Paughco springer, which is steered by 7/8-inch stainless handlebars from Hack's buddy Sawsall.

Hackasaw specializes in clean simple bikes, using parts from a variety of sources.

A 1963 Harley 45 Flathead supplies power.

They sit atop custom dog bone risers. The spike acorn nuts all over the bike were turned up in the shop.

The front wheel is a vintage Hallcraft. It's kept on center by classy ribbed spacers turned in Hackasaw's shop. The front brake is a mostly useless four-inch mini drum.

Rust will not be a big concern on much of this bike. The custom rear brake linkage was formed from stainless. It has Oilite bushings at all pivots to assure smooth actuation.

The custom exhaust pipes are also stainless. They exit the right sides of the cylinders like they're supposed to do, then loop under the bike and blast out beneath the tranny on the left side. They are solidly supported so they will remain reliably attached.

In the spirit of keeping things simple, there is no battery. Electrical needs are fed by a custom mounted Lucas magneto, mounted au naturel. The Prince of Darkness made the Zener diode and rectifier, too. Maybe ol' Joseph Lucas has gotten a bad rap all these years. Ignition is via magneto.

This bike is truly on old school type of build. The parts were gathered over a few months, mocked up as the pile got big enough to do so. Then in a flurry of activity, Hack called his buddies in and had a build party, where most of the work was completed.

Finishing took just a few more days of concentrated effort. The result is a very unique and outstanding bike.

The Donnie Smith-designed Sportster still looks great after all these years. The model is Heather Calcagno.

Two Original Donnie Smith Choppers

With the "discovery" of choppers by cable television producers and audiences, there's been an explosion of sorts among new bike builders, too. Custom bike building is now what one mover and shaker in the TV business described as being mainstream. And with the increasing number of new builders, some of the veteran builders seem to have taken a back seat.

But things aren't necessarily the way they appear. In reality, the more wily veterans are busier than ever, building bikes and selling them as fast as you can say "graybeard." They're just staying out of the spotlight, that's all.

Donnie Smith is among those crafty "old guys." Today's newbies acknowledge him as one of the old masters. They recognize his sense for style in many of his older creations, as if they were the curriculum

for a Choppers 101 class in good taste and detail.

Donnie Smith's early choppers have a look all their own. An astute student of the craft can spot one right away. Such was the case with the sighting of these two beauties. They were both at an indoor show in Ft. Lauderdale.

The Big Twin was spotted first and a quick check of the back end revealed that the bike was indeed from Minnesota, Smith's homeland. That sealed the deal, even before owner Gregor Parochka acknowledged that the bike was indeed an original from Donnie's shop. He then added that he had another one, a Sportster, on the other side of the auditorium.

Now one man owning *two* Donnie Smith original bikes just is not fair; not until every chopper book author owns one anyway. This is a family book, so we

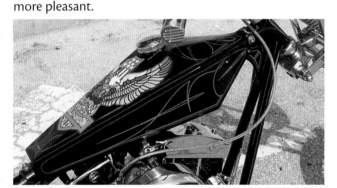

Sp;ortster's swingarm rear suspension makes bumpy roads more pleasant.

Kevin Winter applied the paint lo those many years ago.

1969 XLCH motor is stock and doesn't leak!

won't mention what Gregor is luckier than, but let it be known he's got a heavy streak of it going.

Turns out that Gregor is from the Twin Cities area and has known Donnie and brother Happy most of his life. That's supposed to make it OK that he has two of the bikes. Yeah, whatever.

It's interesting to note that neither of Gregor's bikes has been restored and, even though both are around 30 years old, they still look very good. A few chrome components have been touched up a bit, but that's about it. Both engines have been rebuilt in that time, though.

The Sportster-based bike is built around a 1969 XLCH. The motor was rebuilt by Underground Cycles in Rivera Beach, Florida, using stock H-D

componentry including the Bendix carb. Gregor said he rides the bike a little bit every day.

The real meat of this bike is who fabricated and assembled it originally in St. Paul. That credo belongs to Smith Brothers & Fetrow. The frame is a modified '69 Sportster with stock rear suspension. Hear that, hardcore chopper guys?

The front end is the famous SB&F girder. Those are being remanufactured these days offshore, but out of round tube. The original on this bike is square tube. It's no wonder that front end is highly sought after. It's strong and it's pretty.

Speaking of pretty, check that SB&F long coffin tank. And the taillight, and the rear fender and struts, and on and on. One of the outstanding features of

Big Twin shares the profile that is unmistakably Smith.

Kevin Winter's paint has held up well on the big bike, too.

the bike is the Kevin Winter paint, applied back in the day in St. Paul.

The same theme continues when you move over to look at the Big Twin version. Same Smith Brothers & Fetrow components. Same expert spraying and striping. Another Bates headlight, but mounted under the girder on this one.

The bikes are both unmistakably Donnie Smith bikes, but they are different. This one is based around a 1965 FLH frame *with swingarm*. The engine is a combination of a 1959 lower end and 1966 Shovel top end. It's a stroker, displacing 88-cubic inches and

running Lienweber cams. It was rebuilt by Decoux Engineering in Minneapolis.

Like the Sportster, the Big Twin bike is gorgeous. Both are the types of bikes that you just can't look away from if you're near them. They're just right, obviously designed by someone who loves his job.

Donnie's outlook on motorcycling has always been: "No one has to own a motorcycle. They're a hobby, something to have fun on."

Couldn't agree more, Donnie. Couldn't agree more.

Wassermann 1975 XLCH

This bike could be considered a time machine straight from 1975 except for two major points. One, it has a modern rear disc brake. Two, it was built nearly 30 years *after* 1975.

Obviously, John Wassermann is a student of the old school. When he set out to build this 1975 Harley Sportster-based chopper, he had his eye set on chopper styles of three decades ago. He's a purist with definite ideas of what a proper chopper should entail. One of those features is a kick starter. That's

why he picked the kick-only XLCH model as the basis for his rolling homage to choppers past.

Sportster choppers are certainly nothing new, though they haven't often gotten the kind of attention as the Big Twin bikes have. Fact is, a Sportster packs more performance for the dollar than any other Harley configuration.

Until the introduction of the V-Rod a few years ago, the Sportster was the most powerful model in the Harley lineup. That's a distinction the Sportster

A Lucas headlight with visor.

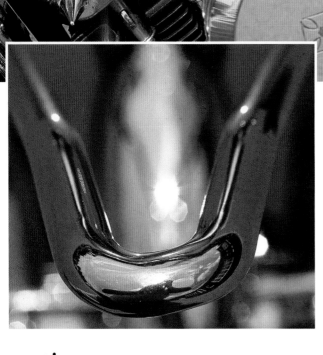

Looks like a spike farm on top of the Ironhead's engine.

John hand-formed the sissy bar.

Forward controls were owner-built.

A perfect, compact engine combo for a chopper.

Paughco fishtails, a chopper standard.

The Sparto chrome taillight always looks good.

has worn since its debut in 1957. They also provide a very compact chopping package because the engine and transmission are one unit. For the chopper builder looking for power and a less-troublesome build, it's just hard to beat a Sportster.

And it's really hard to beat John Wassermann's version. The bike has won the old school chopper and/or Sportster class in nearly every show it has been entered in.

John has defintely captured "the look" on his orange Sporty. In the 1970s, everyone wanted to outdo the next guy on radical front end length and geometry, and this bike's 20-inch-over-stock period springer on a 50-plus-degree rake does the trick. It would not be hard to convince the average onlooker that this chopper was built in 1975 when the bike was new.

The glittering upswept Paughco fishtails are another nod to tradition, one that looks perfectly in character. The gas tank and oil tank also came from Paughco. That's because the traditionalists at Paughco still build them like they did 30 years ago.

The only giveaway to modernity is the GMA disc brake out back on the 16-inch wheel, a wise choice given the brakeless front spool, another period throwback more grounded in appearance than common sense.

This bike is no trailer queen. It gets ridden and ridden hard. John often rides it back and forth to his job as a Ford dealership mechanic. That's another old school aspect of John's relationship to his bike. Old school guys didn't usually build their bikes to be show-only. They rode them, often daily. So what if the paint got a chip? It's a motorcycle, not a display object.

Flanders bars sit atop dogbone risers.

Wear gloves when you clean this bike.

MISTRESS
BY
WASSERMANN

Honesty is the best policy.

Brake? We don't need no stinkin' brake!

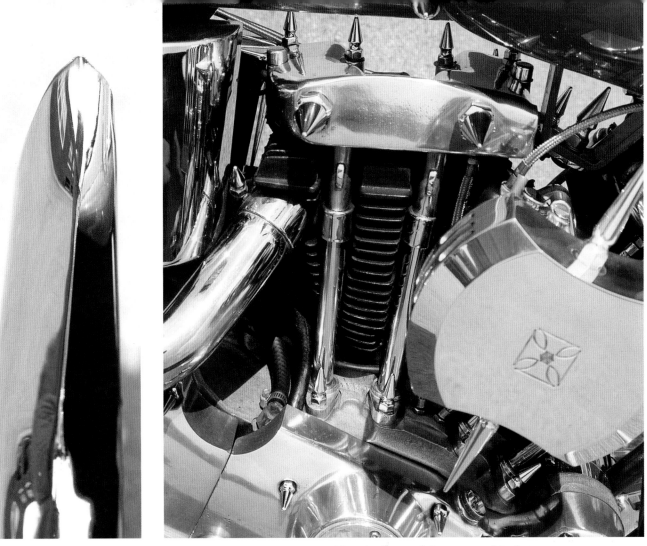

There's plenty of chrome on this chopper.

Matt Brandon hand-made the near-seamless air cleaner.

Don Richie painted John's bike and it would be hard to pick a more appropriate color than the House of Kolor pearl orange. Did you see that air cleaner? Matt Brandon cranked that out on a Bridgeport *manual* milling machine. It's made up of several aluminum pieces, yet appears almost seamless. He also crafted the footpegs.

You may have noticed there are a few spikes on the bike. Tony Sanders was the spike chucker, making most of the sharp pointed objects for the rocker box, front axle and rear end. John says there are over 210 spikes on the bike all together. He loses count.

Other than the chrome plating and a few of the other small components, John built the chopper at home in his own garage. That's what helped him accomplish another old school feat—keeping the cost down to a minimum.

John says he has less than $2,500 in actual cash invested in the bike. Start with an inexpensive base and do most of the work personally and the cost for a head-turning chopper can be very reasonable.

Shane Masters' Bargain Chop

This is about as clean a chop as you'll find.

What will $25,000 buy in a custom motorcycle these days? It would buy one factory-built semi-custom bike like a year-old American Ironhorse or Big Dog. Or it would buy 10 bikes like Shane Masters' 1972 Ironhead Sportster.

Ten? Yes, 10. Shane says he has exactly $2,465 wrapped up in this bike.

How did he do that? Riddle me this, Batman: the answer is in the question. He did it, as in himself and not someone else. Shane's own hours were free, so he didn't have to pay for them. That's how to get such a sweet bike for such little money – do it yourself.

As noted, the bike is a 1972 Harley Sportster, fondly called the Ironhead because – ta da – the heads are cast iron.

The Ironhead makes one of the slickest packages around for the basis of a chopper. As noted in another chapter, the Sportster package is a chopper

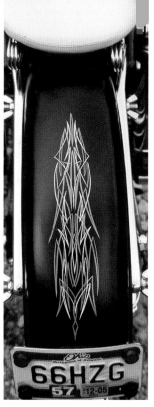

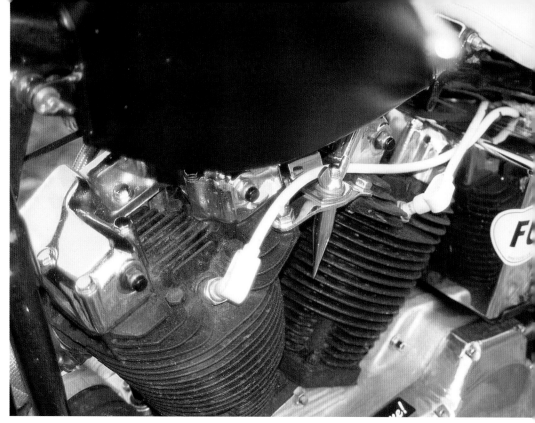

White pinstriping accents the black pieces.

Ironhead Sportsters have iron heads.

Shocks smooth the ride and the seat's a swap meet find.

Chrome won't get ya home. It'll get ya looks, though.

Copper flake frame is by Pat Patterson.

builder's dream. It's one unit as opposed to the Big Twin's separate transmission and engine.

Additionally, it's a very good-looking engine; very basic and mechanical in appearance, styled much like the Shovelhead Big Twins.

The Sportster was the hot rod Harley of the era, too. Sportsters were always the fastest and quickest of the lot. That gives the builder a leg up on a chopper or bobber build right out of the gate.

Shane maintained much of the original bike in his build. He chopped off the unnecessary pieces for his chopper, lightened others, and enhanced the mechanicals. Technically the bike could probably be called a bobber. This is one that straddles the line between chopper and bobber, but seems to be a mild chopper, mostly because of the final look and stance.

It's a judgment call, OK?

Mechanically, the engine got a Shane rebuild. He did a little mild porting while things were apart and dropped in some Andrews cams. The carb is the ever-popular S&S Super E. The tranny is stock, too.

Guys who build non-Sportster choppers have been putting Sporty tanks on them since, uh, probably since there have been Sporty tanks. So

it makes sense to keep the Sportster tank on a Sportster chopper.

That's what Shane did. The frame is stock, too, and even retains the swingarm. That makes things a lot more comfy on the pothole riddled streets around Shane's Dayton, Ohio, home.

What's not stock about those parts is the paint. Pat Patterson, owner of Led Sled Customs, sprayed the new color. In a twist from the usual practice (and twists from usual practice are the usual practice at Led Sled), Pat painted the frame in copper metalflake and the tank, oil tank, and reworked stock rear fender in matte black. Then all those black parts were tastefully pinstriped.

The white swap meet seat enhances and complements the whole shebang. Handlebars are pullbacks and the small 4-1/2-inch headlight fits the package. The front forks were overhauled at Forking by Frank. The brakes are the good-looking stock Harley drums.

Whitewall Avon tires complete the whole look on this fine low-budget ride. It should inspire the bargain builder in us all.

Frank Skiba's Ariel Square Four

Ariel Square Four chopper is a classy looking bike.

Lynwood, California's, Frank Skiba knows that his chopper can have a polarizing effect in some crowds. See, it's an Ariel Square Four.

Ariels are highly sought-after prizes in the world of antique motorcycles. When some of the resto guys see one made into a chopper, it sets their nerves on edge just a tad. Frank has come to expect such reactions and he just lets the guys rant for awhile. Then they skulk off and take their nerve pills and things are back to normal again.

Frank didn't build the bike; a guy named Geno did. So this perceived sacrilege is not really Frank's fault. Give the man a break.

See Chapter 10 for more background on Ariel Square Fours. The Ariel's compact engine design was tailor-made for chopper use. That compact, square lump fits right into a chopper frame and makes for a powerful and distinctive package.

Geno reports that Frank Bonneville rebuilt the 1958 engine for the bike. It still retains the stock

Ariel Square Four is one of the most distinctive engines of all time.

The girder is a modified aftermarket production unit

Two pipes per size are Siamesed into one.

Even the logo looks classy.

A Vertex magneto provides the spark.

The front spoke wheel uses a Hallcraft brake.

Geno built the peaked tank.

Rear suspension is the traditional British plunger-style.

1000 cc displacement and utilizes flat-top pistons. Valley Head Service reworked the heads. A single Amal carburetor feeds the four cylinders. There is no air cleaner. Geno made the custom Siamesed pipes. Ignition fire comes from a Vertex magneto.

The two decades of continuous Ariel engine improvements by the British factory culminated in 1958, the last year of Square Four production, so this bike's engine is the best of the breed. The bike still has 6-volt electrics.

As might be expected, a potential chopper builder cannot just whip open a catalog and order a chopper frame for an Ariel Square Four. So Geno did what any enterprising fabricator would do – he built

his own. About eight inches of extra stretch was incorporated into the backbone, along with an extra three degrees of rake.

The girder front end is an EME that was modified to meet this bike's needs. Geno built the peaked gas tank and installed a five-quart oil tank to keep the Square Four well lubricated. Risers are three inches high. Geno also made the foot pegs. Seat, too.

A Hallcraft front brake is used on the 21-inch front-spoked wheel. A stock Ariel drum brake does duty out back.

The maroon paint color seems right for this bike. It's understated and classy, just like this sweet-sounding bike.

Thin is in for old time chopper fans.

Tennessee Triumph

Sean Mahoney seems to have a knack for cranking out some great Triumph choppers. Must be his Irish heritage coupled with the British iron. Whatever it is, this Triumph is a beaut.

A Nashville, Tennessee, area resident, Sean has the energy of three men and he'll wear you out just trying to keep up with him.

He does residential title searches for a living, but he is also an amateur boxer, has a band (Johnny Gringo) and runs the Southern Fried Choppers chopper builder Web forums. Whew!

This particular Triumph has a 1960 pre-unit drivetrain. For those not Triumph-savvy, that means the engine and transmission are separate units, much as a Big Twin Harley is. After 1962, Triumph went to unit construction with the engine and transmission in the same case. Both types have their fans. Most hardcore Triumph guys like them both. The transmission is a Triumph Slickshift.

The assistance of Chuck Skarsuane was enlisted for the engine rebuild. See Chuck's own Triumph in the next chapter of this book. Chuck is an active member of the SFC forums as are others who offered assistance and/or advice.

Sean lists the "Prince of Darkness" as providing the ignition. That's one Mr. Joseph Lucas to you who haven't experienced Brit bike electrics. Carb is standard issue Amal. There is no air cleaner, just a J.J. Walker velocity stack. The high exit, swoopy pipes were made by Sean.

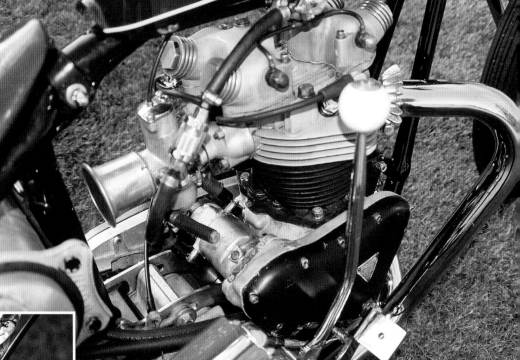

Pre-unit Triumph powertrain is from 1960.

Springer is a vintage AEE Choppers piece.

Long, sweeping exhaust pipes were Sean's creation.

Jason North is responsible for the paint.

The spun aluminum oil tank is by Moon.

The Bultaco mini-drum slows things down a little.

That pre-unit combo was wedged into a 1952 Triumph rigid frame that has been treated to a little rake and a little stretch. Hung midway in that frame is a genuine Moon oil tank.

Fabrication duties on the Triumph's build were a joint effort between Sean and Jason North. Jason was also the painter and laid down some gorgeous red metalflake, trimmed in black and accented with classic pinstripes.

Sean agrees that real choppers don't have front fenders, but the rear fender is a cut-down trailer fender. The fuel tank is from a Sportster. The red metal flake seat from Fat Lucky's has white stitching to mimic the pinstripes.

Sean also seems to have a talent for finding obscure parts and making them work together. Witness the Bultaco mini-drum front brake laced to the Akront 21-inch rim. The front end is an old AEE springer, which seems to be as rare as hen's teeth, especially when you consider how many must have been sold back in the day.

The rear tire is a Goodyear MT90, wrapped around a Harley rim, in turn wrapped around a stock Triumph hub.

Atop the springer, find mini-bike risers holding twisted Z-bars. The headlight came from Russell Delffs. Real choppers do have taillights. This one is a bright LED, all the better to keep some four-wheeler driver at bay on a dark Tennessee night.

Long and lean in Bowling Green.

Bowling Green Triumph

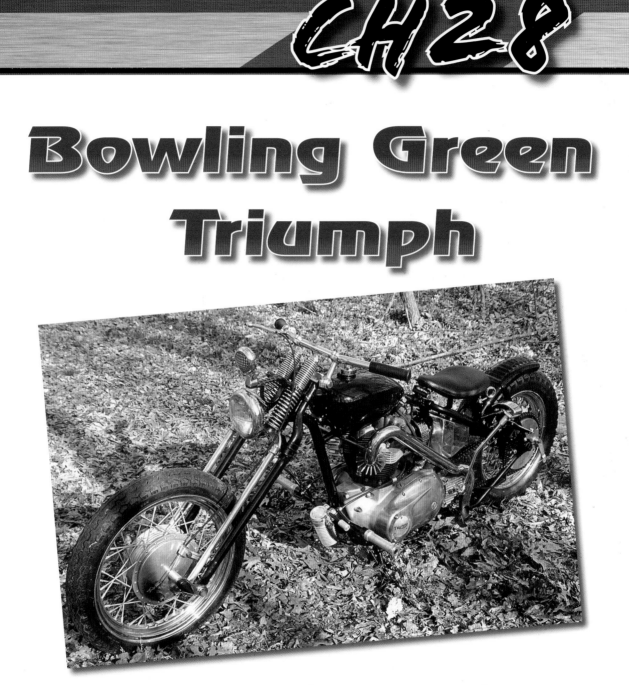

Chuck Skarsaune's Triumph is exemplary of why hardcore chopper guys love Triumphs so much. It is light and lean and has that gorgeous twin sitting out there for all to see.

Choppers are all about the engine and as little else as possible besides. Old Triumphs are all about the engine. They are the basic motorcycle containing just enough components to support the engine and rider and make them go down the road.

By day, Chuck is a manufacturing engineer at RC Components in Bowling Green, Kentucky. RC manufactures high quality parts for flashy customs. By night, he toils away in his own garage shop, cranking out bare-bones chops like this one, and a few sundry parts for his buddies' similarly basic rides. Flashy pays the bills but basic moves the blood.

Sportster brakes do the job.

Forward controls are homemade.

The seat is comfy for long Kentucky rides.

Choppers 101 – use what you have.

The shift knob was once a steering adjuster.

Polished stainless pipes were bent by Chuck at home.

Ribbed spacers were made in Chuck's garage.

Chuck and his buddy Sawsall took a '71 Triumph frame and goose-necked it, stretched it about six inches and added a hardtail.

The rear fender is punched full o' louvers. This is a real chopper, so there is no front fender. The front end is a springer of unknown parentage that Chuck took four inches out of. It's topped off by drag bars on dog bone risers.

The '71 T120R engine has been bored .040 inches over stock. It's mostly stock Triumph otherwise with '63 heads using later valves. Mr. Lucas no longer completely controls the spark, though. Ignition is Boyer and Podtronics enhanced now.

Chuck built his own forward controls and jockey shift. In keeping with its Spartan nature, the bike has minimal bright work. One exception: the owner-bent stainless high pipes.

Some oft-overlooked wheels and brakes were added to the mix, ones from a 1965 Harley Sportster. They look good and work great on a light bike like this one. They have the right style in that they look like they came from the 1960s.

Too many builders mix and match parts from different eras that don't look right together. The result is a hodge-podge with no flow, no style.

This Mr. Sins-painted Trump ("Black like motorcycles are supposed to be," says Chuck) sits way low, which comes in handy on the curvy roads surrounding Chuck's house in the sticks. You'd be hard pressed to find better roads to ride a motorcycle on than the ones right around Bowling Green.

The gas tank is a British peanut tank and the oil tank is a horseshoe style. The headlight is an old, but classy Unity Equipe version.

Kim Wroblewski's Triumph and More

The sum of the parts of Kim Wroblewski's Triumph is awesome.

OK. You should know up front that this Triumph-based bike defies description. It's transmogrified, that's what it is! This thing is a conglomeration of parts from all kinds of different bikes – Triumph, KTM, Ducati, Kawasaki – all carefully mixed with an artful eye. Oh yeah, it's drop dead gorgeous, too.

Kim Wroblewski is a motorcycle nut. Honda CBX, BSA Firebird Scrambler, Triumph Trident, Ducati Monster – those and many more are all part of his collection. He has bikes in his garage that

would make anyone drool… especially a guy writing a book about motorcycles. But enough of that.

When Kim decided he wanted a custom Triumph, he looked at things a little differently than the average Joe Chopper. The Triumph T-120 Bonneville power plant was a given, but he wanted a bike that would handle and ride well on the roads near his Avon, Indiana, home.

A swing arm was on the menu. He sketched out a plan and took it to Jason Hart at Chopsmiths in

Bars are tapered aluminum KTM/Renthal.

The fender is massaged WCC; the taillight is from a 1966 Triumph.

Forks are KYB motocross style from a Kawasaki.

The front brake's are Nissin caliper grips SuperMotard disc.

The stack feeds a 32 mm Mikuni carb.

Joe Hunt magneto drives off the side of a Bonneville engine.

Indianapolis. Jason looked at Kim like he had three eyes, but he was open to Kim's suggestion. Got a business to run, you know?

The fact that Jason and Kim have a highly respected mutual friend probably helped the idea sell. Roy Caruthers is a well-known motorcycle and hot rod builder in the Indianapolis area. He hangs out at Jason's shop sometimes (when there's beer in the fridge) and he also assisted Kim in building his bike.

The plan was to use a 1974 Bonneville's engine cradle and build a stretched custom swingarm frame around that. The result was a 10-inch stretch in the oil-holding backbone and three inches in the downtube. Rake is 41 degrees. They crafted a custom four-inch over stock swingarm to go with it.

While Jason was working on the frame, Kim dove into the engine rebuild. He used Hepolite pistons and MegaCycle cams. While the engine was apart, Kim did a mild porting job, and then installed Black Diamond valves with bronze guides. SW springs use alloy retainers. The carburetors are 32 mm Mikunis wearing velocity stacks.

Kim made the exhaust headers and mated them to Jemco flat track megaphones. The pipe heat shields are from a Ducati.

Kim likes the look of a Triumph fuel tank, but the stretched frame required that the tank be stretched as well. The front fender is a hand-rolled aluminum piece while the rear is a heavily-modified West Coast Choppers fender.

Homemade pipes wear Ducati guards.

A man used to riding modern European bikes likes some stopping power on his vintage machines, too. A Nissin caliper on a 320 mm Braking Super Motard disc does the duty extremely well in front. Another Nissin caliper on an EBC disc handles the rear stoppage.

Sweet handling depends a lot on the forks, so KYB inverted MX forks from a Kawasaki were installed in the Triumph neck. The handlebars are tapered aluminum KTM/Renthal bars atop Scott billet risers. The steering damper once lived on a Ducati. Out back, Works Performance billet shocks absorb the bumps.

Wheels are a combination of black Excel rims laced to powder coated Kawasaki hubs. Joining the two are stainless steel spokes.

Kim handled his own electrical work, creating a harness linking to a Tympanium unit with a capacitor. There is no battery and the bike starts on the first kick. The headlight is from a 1966 Triumph, to which a prewar switch plate has been grafted. The taillight is cast alloy, also from a '66 Triumph.

Chopsmiths created the custom seat pan and it received a Stitches cover. Kim performed the painting duties on the bike. A black basecoat was followed by silver pearl, gold fade, and gray pinstripe, all in House of Kolor paints. Urethane clear coat seals it all in smoothly.

All this sounds like a bizarre mix if you haven't seen the bike. Kim says, "When I took the concept to Chopsmiths, Jason was not immediately a convert to the Triumph plan. With his talents on the frame fab, the overall result is exactly what I was after."

SECTION FOUR:
WRAP-UP

The Shop in Ventura, CA, has a roof full of vintage Indian and Harley frames.

Part of WTTM's bobber display includes a collection of fishtail exhaust tips.

Any wonder why WTTM is called the "Museum That Runs?"

Ventura Motorworks' Kurt Morrow does everything from engine builds to fabrication to assembly.

Keeping the Flame Burning

Ventura Motorworks is well-versed in Indian (& Harley) choppers and bobbers.

True bobbers and choppers are an obsession for those who really love them. They are not for everyone, though. Most motorcycle riders prefer the modern conveniences of windshields, turn signals, and saddlebags, electric starters and warranties. No bobbers or choppers will have all of those. Most will have none.

Bobbers are custom motorcycles at their most minimal. In some ways, they are a throwback to a much simpler time, a return to basics. They consist of few parts and the entire parts list could be hand-written on the back of an envelope. Engine, frame, wheel assemblies, tank, seat, back fender, lights, forks, handlebars, controls, oil tank and wires. That's about it. Most have a paint job; some do not.

Bobbers' simplicity is their beauty. For someone who loves the mechanical aspect of a motorcycle, bobbers are it. Most newer production bikes on the market have plastic fairings and ductwork, plastic fenders, lots of extra gee-gaws that detract from the brutal beauty of the basic motorcycle. The bobber eschews all that and goes to the bare minimum. In nearly all cases, bobbers are built for one rider. If there is a provision for a passenger, it will be extremely minimal.

Remember, bobbers were born of the need for speed, outgrowths of street bikes cum race bikes, ridden by men with a yearning to go fast and no need to carry extra weight. If you start dressing up a bobber, you have created something else. A bobber has been bobbed. It starts out bigger and fatter than it ends up. Those are the rules.

Choppers are a little different. Choppers by definition have been chopped, which isn't all that much different from bobbing, except that it doesn't usually stop there. Choppers are about style, so they are more

Simple yet striking, Dave Shoemaker's Triumph is a bobber done right.

Choppers can be elegant; witness Mark Hannah's Panhead.

likely to get some extra chrome, a longer front end, flashier wheels and paint, a sissy bar, maybe a king and queen seat, some molding on the frame. All those things add weight and none enhance performance. Choppers are about lookin' good – stylin'.

Still, it's a means of self-expression. No two choppers are alike, even ones built by the same builder. Leave the mass production and interchangeable parts to Eli Whitney and Henry Ford. Individuality means one-off. Riders of choppers will never mistake their bikes for someone else's in a huge Bike Week parking lot. No sir, one of kind all around.

Parts is parts

Since chopper and bobber builders like their bikes to be different from the next guy's, there aren't a great many off-the-shelf chopper components available.

That would defeat the purpose, now wouldn't it? There are a few, though, and some of them have been around a long, long time. Your local independent motorcycle shop can probably get parts from most of these suppliers. Some will sell directly to the consumer.

One of the best-known and oldest suppliers of new chopper and bobber components is Paughco. Paughco sells frames, springer front ends, gas tanks, exhaust pipes and many more parts as well. Their quality is good and the prices reasonable. They have been in business since 1969 and still produce many of the same components they made over 30 years ago.

Another familiar name is Jammer Cycle Products. Jammer was around in the 1970s and they're back with some cool old school parts, accessories and rolling chassis.

A well-equipped shop's basic machinery. This is Ventura Motorworks.

Small shops like Chandler Originals crank out some excellent, affordable choppers.

Some of the better known "production bobber and chopper" builders also have some pretty cool components that more and more chopper/bobber builders are incorporating into their builds. Those include Exile Cycles, Sucker Punch Sally's, and Flyrite Choppers. As an example, both Flyrite and Exile make a combination rear brake rotor and sprocket. Such a piece can go a long way toward simplifying a motorcycle's rear wheel area.

Tires are an important part of the look of a chopper or bobber. Since classic chops and bobbers often utilize old wheels rather than the currently in-vogue fat hoops, it may be a little difficult to find the right tires.

That's especially true if you're looking for wide whitewalls in a specific size or tires with traditional tread patterns. Never fear, Coker is here. Coker Tire

most likely has you covered and they'll have the tires in stock to boot.

Speaking of tires, in reference to the current trend of huge back tires on so-called choppers – just say "no." Enough said.

Shops for your chops

Not everyone has the skills, time, talent or tools to build a kick-ass chopper or bobber. We would all like to be able to do so, but it ain't in the cards. Do not lose heart. There are motorcycle shops out there that are staffed by people who think like you do. You can get a real chopper or bobber, built by real bikers, and it won't necessarily cost you an arm and a leg.

There is a partial list of such shops in the final chapter of this book. It is in no way complete. Ask around in your area of the country to find out who has a good reputation with the other bikers. Word of

Hank Young is one of the masters at building pretty period-correct bikes

Led Sled Customs in Dayton is one of the innovative rising star chopper shops.

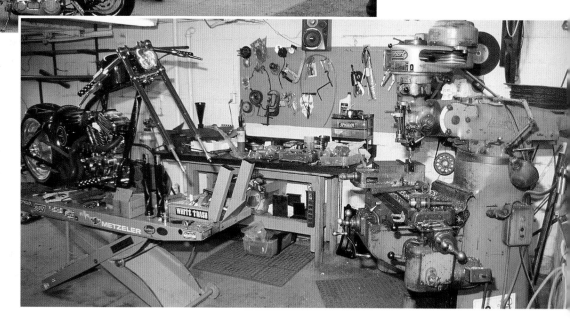

Led Sled's lower level shop is well-equipped for all needs.

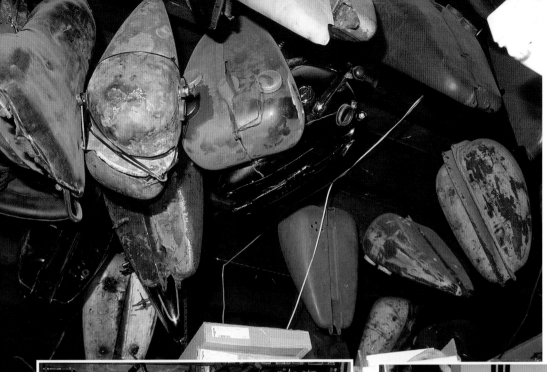

The Shop's supply of vintage tanks is pretty impressive, too.

Mike Silvio built this period-correct bobber for his Cyclemo's Museum.

Wheels Through Time Museum has one display devoted to original early bobbers.

mouth will be a good gauge of the shop's worthiness for your project.

And speaking of local bike shops, build a relationship with one. It might be tempting to buy parts from a mail order or Internet supplier, but a face-to-face relationship with a competent local bike shop can be invaluable. Buy your tires, oil, and other regular needs from them. If they are a dealer for the parts you're after, buy through the local guy. It keeps him in business for when you really need him, it helps the local economy, and it gives you a place to hang out, too.

Biker friendly museums

You probably noticed that many of the motorcycles featured in this book are from the Wheels Through Time Museum in Maggie Valley, North Carolina. That's because the museum, owned by Dale Walksler, has the finest collection of American motorcycles in the US. Period. And Dale is not a purist. He owns bobbers and choppers and he builds them, too.

What makes the whole deal even better is that Dale is so savvy when it comes to the history of all aspects of American motorcycles that he knows exactly what a modified bike from a specific era (or geographical area) should look like. The man is a walking encyclopedia. Visit him and learn.

Not all that far from Wheels Through Time lies another small town treasure trove, albeit on a smaller

Only three magazines regularly feature old school bikes. *The Horse* is the best of the three.

but growing scale. Red Boiling Springs, Tennessee, is home to Cyclemo's Motorcycle Museum. Owner Mike Silvio is pretty knowledgeable in his own right and is just as passionate as Dale Walksler about the subject at hand.

Both Cyclemo's and WTTM are wall-to-wall with vintage American motorcycles, advertising items, signs, apparel…you name it. Either is a destination well worth a trip. If you live outside the area, make a journey of it and go to both.

Other resources

It's a little hard to believe, but none of the remaining early chopper magazines have stayed true to the basic chopper and bobber cause. Most have succumbed to the high dollar advertisers and the bikes wearing their overpriced, gaudy componentry.

There is one exception and I don't name it as such simply because I work there, but *The Horse Back Street Choppers* magazine is the one chopper magazine that caters exclusively to the homebuilt

and basic chopper or bobber rider. Some of the other chopper magazines cover that type of bike along with the high buck, fat tired, new catalog parts exclusively versions. Those include most significantly, *Street Chopper* and *Iron Works*.

There are also a few online message boards that offer builders an opportunity to exchange ideas and opinions. Chief among those – *The Horse's* boards (www.ironcross.net) and Jockey Journal (www.jockeyjournal.com).

It's a wrap

In no way can the subject of choppers and bobbers be completely covered in a 176-page book. Ten times that many pages might get a good start. The motorcycles are as varied as the people who build, own and ride them. That's the beauty of them. Like a painting or a sculpture, each one is a work of art.

The art may appeal to many or only to the creator. It doesn't matter; the art has been created.

Old School Resources

Builders & Parts Suppliers

American Legend Motorcycles, Inc.
Lexington, KY
888-272-9143
www.legendmcs.com

Bad Monkey Motorworks
Columbia, SC
803-699-3288
www.badmonkeymotorworks.com

Broadway Choppers
Schenectady, NY
518-374-0008
www.broadwaychoppers.com

Chandler Originals
Lake Worth, FL
561-540-2500
www.chandleroriginals.com

Choppahead
Boston, MA
www.choppahead.com

Chopper Dave's Casting Co.
Long Beach, CA
www.chopperdaves.com

Chopperhead Road
Jacksonville, NC
910-938-0360
www.chopperheadroad.com

Chopsmith's
Indianapolis, IN
317-246-7737
www.handbuiltmotorcycles.com

Coker Tire
Chattanooga, TN
800-251-6336
www.coker.com

Crime Scene Choppers
Scotts Valley, CA
831-406-0126
www.crimescenechoppers.com

Exile Cycles
N. Hollywood, CA
818-255-3330
www.exilecycles.com

Fabricator Kevin's Steel Chopper Parts
Clinton Township, MI

586-291-4798
www.fabkevin.com

Flyrite Choppers
Austin, TX
512-918-CHOP
www.flyritechoppers.com

Hank Young Choppers & Hot Rods
Marietta, GA
770-425-1305
www.youngchoppers.com

Indian Larry Legacy
Brooklyn, NY
718-609-9184
www.indianlarry.com

Jammer Products
Morgan Hill, CA
800-597-6467
www.jammerclub.com

Klockwerks
Mitchell, SD
605-996-3700
www.kustomcycles.com

Led Sled Customs
Dayton, OH
937-879-4645
www.ledsledcustoms.com

Mills & Co.
Marietta, GA
www.millscustoms.com

Music City Motorcycles
Nashville, TN
615-963-9508

Nash Motorcycle
Vancouver, WA
360-693-4225
www.nashmotorcycle.com

Paughco
Carson City, NV
800-423-2621
www.paughco.com

R.E.D. Racing
Boca Raton, FL
561-338-5755
www.redracing.us

Redneck Engineering
Liberty, SC
864-843-3001
www.redneckengenuity.com

Salinas Boys Customs
Salinas, CA
831-424-7753
www.salinasboys.com

Smiley's Bobbers, Choppers & Hot Rods
Lake Worth, FL
561-296-7779
www.smileyschops.com

Stevenson's Cycles
Wayne, MI
734-641-2200
www.stevensonscycle.com

Sucker Punch Sally's
Cincinnati, OH
513-353-1446
www.suckerpunchsallys.com

Sully's Old School Customs
Centerville, IN
765-855-5307
www.sullivansmotorcycles.com

The Shop
Ventura, CA
805-650-6777
www.cycleshop.com

Ventura Motorworks
Ventura, CA
805-643-7366

Visionary Customs
Hartsville, TN
615-374-9709
www.hackasaw.com

Voodoo Choppers
Rochester, MI
248-601-3000
www.voodoochoppers.com

XsSpeed Choppers
Olsey, MD
301-260-9515
www.xsspeedchoppers,com

Museums

Cyclemo's Motorcycle Museum
Red Boiling Springs, TN
615-699-5049
www.cyclemos.com

Wheels Through Time All American Transportation Museum
Maggie Valley, NC
828-926-6266
www.wheelsthroughtime.com

Magazines

The Horse Back Street Choppers
www.thehorsemag.com

IronWorks
www.ironworksmag.com

Street Chopper
www.streetchopperweb.com

More Books on

Big Bold Bikes

Anatomy of the Chopper

by Doug Mitchel

Chopper fan or customizing expert, there's a lot for you to love in this beautiful chopper book. Page after page of stunning professional studio photos of more than 30 styles of customized motorcycles fill this inspiring and entertaining bike guide. The 350 color photos reveal the master craftsmanship and artistry surrounding bike building of yesterday, and today.

The popularity of choppers is undeniable, and this book illustrates the design and construction of a modern chopper. In addition, you'll discover background details about the designers and companies represented, and a valuable builder contact list in the back of the book. Among the bike builders and companies featured are:

- Russel Mitchell and Exile Cycles
- Rich "Pyro" Pollack
- BREW Bikes LLC
- Kingpin Cycles
- Warren Lane

A great gift for every chopper owner or fan of these cutting-edge two-wheel titans, *Anatomy of the Chopper* pays homage to the craft, character and chrome of chopper building like nothing else!

Hardcover • 10-3/4 x 10-3/4 • 256 pages
350 color photos
Item# ACHPR • $34.99

Eddie Paul's Extreme Chopper Building

Real Techniques for Outrageous Results
by Eddie Paul

Learn key chopper building techniques from expert customizer Eddie Paul as he revamps a Boss Hoss motorcycle into a radical ride. More than 250 brilliant color photos.

Softcover • 8-1/4 x 10-7/8 • 176 pages
250+ color photos
Item# RXCBD • $24.99

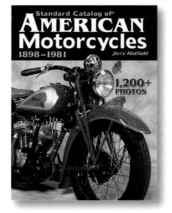

Standard Catalog of® American Motorcycles 1898-1981

The Only Book to Fully Chronicle Every Bike Ever Built
by Jerry H. Hatfield

Rediscover the reasons you love your favorite model of motorcycle with the help of 1,200 photos, and historical details featured in this comprehensive guide to American-made motorcycles.

Softcover • 8-1/2 x 11 • 448 pages
1,200 b&w photos
Item# ACYL • $29.99

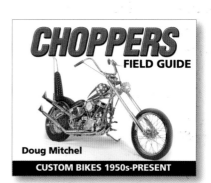

Choppers Field Guide

Custom Bikes 1950s-Present
by Doug Mitchel

Explore 70 different custom choppers from the 1950s to today, in 250+ intricate photos of the chrome, paint, engines and custom touches that make these specialty bikes unique.

Softcover • 5-3/16 x 4-3/16 • 408 pages
250 color photos
Item# CHPFG • $12.99

Get your copy of these radical references today! Available from booksellers and other retailers nationwide or directly from Krause Publications by calling 800-258-0929 Offer AUB6 or online at www.krausebooks.com

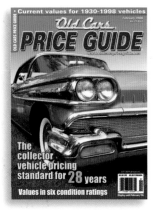